THROUGH THEIR EYES

TOMORROW'S VOICES

Edited By Sarah Waterhouse

First published in Great Britain in 2020 by:

Young Writers
Remus House
Coltsfoot Drive
Peterborough
PE2 9BF
Telephone: 01733 890066
Website: www.youngwriters.co.uk

All Rights Reserved
Book Design by Ashley Janson
© Copyright Contributors 2019
Softback ISBN 978-1-83928-787-9

Printed and bound in the UK by BookPrintingUK
Website: www.bookprintinguk.com
YB0433J

FOREWORD

Since 1991, here at Young Writers we have celebrated the awesome power of creative writing, especially in young adults, where it can serve as a vital method of expressing strong (and sometimes difficult) emotions, a conduit to develop empathy, and a safe, non-judgemental place to explore one's own place in the world. With every poem we see the effort and thought that each pupil published in this book has put into their work and by creating this anthology we hope to encourage them further with the ultimate goal of sparking a life-long love of writing.

Through Their Eyes challenged young writers to open their minds and pen bold, powerful poems from the points-of-view of any person or concept they could imagine – from celebrities and politicians to animals and inanimate objects, or even just to give us a glimpse of the world as they experience it. The result is this fierce collection of poetry that by turns questions injustice, imagines the innermost thoughts of influential figures or simply has fun.

The nature of the topic means that contentious or controversial figures may have been chosen as the narrators, and as such some poems may contain views or thoughts that, although may represent those of the person being written about, by no means reflect the opinions or feelings of either the author or us here at Young Writers.

We encourage young writers to express themselves and address subjects that matter to them, which sometimes means writing about sensitive or difficult topics. If you have been affected by any issues raised in this book, details on where to find help can be found at *www.youngwriters.co.uk/info/other/contact-lines*

CONTENTS

Furness Academy, Barrow-In-Furness

Elly-May Parsons (12)	1
Niamh Marr (13)	2
Lydia-Hope Hill (15)	4
Amelia Leach (12)	6
Shana McMullan (13)	8
Ella Benson (12)	10
Angel Joanna Beckman (11)	12
Michael Milby (13)	13
Ashlee Dickinson (13)	14
Daniel Nicholson (12)	16
Nathan Boyes (13)	17
Kayley Blezard (11)	18
Harry McMurdo (13)	19
Holly Warbrick (13)	20
Violet Mae Bland (11)	21
Christos Smargiannakis (12)	22
Theo Christopher Powell (13)	23
Lacey Smith (13)	24
Brooke Smith-Hadwick (13)	25
Lexi-Mia Grove (12)	26
Seth Mills (12)	27
Freddie Lawton (13)	28
Mabel Vernon Charles (11)	29
Ruby Palmer (14)	30
Demi Rawlinson (13)	31
Keiron Egerton (13)	32
Bailey McLaughlin (13)	33
Jack O'Neill (13)	34
Steph Carter (14)	35
Macy McArthur (11)	36
Amelia Massey Holmes (11)	37
Daniel Keay (12)	38
Jamie-Leigh Thorley (12)	39

Charlie Bo Caine (12)	40
Charlie Morgan (12)	41
Keira Shand-Lupton (13)	42
Jack Whittall (13)	43
Tia Mullen (11)	44
Nikita Wilding (12)	45
Lauren Hewson (12)	46
Maddie Shepherd (12)	47
Zachary James Downing (12)	48
Emily Miller (12)	49
Khian Joseph Phizacklea Powell (13)	50
Ella Moon (12)	51
Finlay Crompton (12)	52
Joshua Brown (12)	53

Handsworth Wood Girls' Academy, Birmingham

Aimee Caulkin (13)	54
Suliana Bahta (11)	57
Andreja Elijosiute	58
Isma Rahiem (14)	60

Interhigh School, Crickhowell

Lael Lopez (17)	62
Katie Riley (13)	64
Fiza Iqbal (17)	66
Sara Mughal (12)	67
Yusuf Naveed Khan (15)	68
Yashodah Moodley (12)	69

Lady Aisha Academy, Barking

Zahra Amjad (11)	70
Ammarah Talati (12)	72
Faridah Kaniz Zaman (11)	75
Saniya Bint Ibrahim (12)	76
Bushra Mariam Zaheer (11)	78
Maariya Islam (11)	80
Momina Khan (12)	82
Alizay Shah (12)	83
Zaina Ali (12)	84
Zaynah Bint-Sheraz (11)	85
Aisha Mohammed (12)	86
Khadijah Begum (12)	87
Ruqayyah Zahra Siddiq (11)	88
Laaibah Rashid (11)	89
Hawa Haydari (11)	90
Yasmin Abdul-Ghani (11)	91
Izma Khatun (11)	92
Halima Noor (11)	93
Zikra Mirza (11)	94
Manha Marzuqah Khan (11)	95
Halima Siddika (12)	96

Sedgehill School, Lewisham

Constantinos Kandylakis	97
David Kirinya-Scott Lamont (13)	98
Martin Lamont (15)	100
Ava Annis Klara Drew (13)	102
Maria Binzaru	104
Tetsuya Nicholson (14)	106

The Ramsey Academy, Halstead

Isabel Harris (11)	108
Jessica Goodchild (13)	110
Araya Jackson (13)	112
Tetti Hazell (12)	114
Ellie Chatten (14)	116
Cameron March (11)	118
Jessica Eleanor Tyler (11)	119
Iris Mary Rose Stovell (12)	120
Erin Parry-Jones (12)	122
Samuel Alexander Farnes (13)	123
Courtney Marie Sloat (13)	124
Henry Dale (13)	126
Lily-Rose Collins (13)	128
William Couttie (12)	130
Jacob Cutts (11)	131
Sophie Louise Taylor (12)	132
Tegan Jackson (12)	134
Harry Clark (12)	136
Ella Masterson (15)	137
Tallulah-Mae Kelsey (13)	138
Ellis James Owen Clark (13)	140
Erin Eva Rose Smith (12)	141
Anthony Cook (11)	142
Brandon Jones (12)	143
Ben Turner-Downey (14)	144
Finley Tidbury (12)	146
Emma Eddison (12)	147
Amy Lucas (12)	148
Cian Moore (11)	149
Eddie Naylor (12)	150
Olivia Burlong (13)	151
Katie Elsey (13)	152
Jack William Lewis (11)	153
Zachary Dale (12)	154
Isabelle Talbot (11)	155
Brooke Sparks (14)	156
Ashleigh Taylor-Green (12)	157
Brooke Page (13)	158
Grace D. J. Rawlings (12)	159
Rubee Ceri Creighton (12)	160
Katie Rose (12)	161
Miles Maher-Blyton (12)	162
Bradley Chapman (13)	163
Sonny Stokes-Shinn	164
Natalie Pepper (13)	165
Holli Dixey (11)	166
Hannah Jacob (12)	167
Katie Yallop (12)	168
Reuben Lovell (12)	169
Harry Shelton (12)	170
William Alen	171
Kacey Clements (13)	172

Lilly-Mae Cain (13)	173
Holly Miller (11)	174
Isobel Baxter-Deera (12)	175
Izzy Willsher (13)	176
Darcey Hurst (12)	177
Sennen Root (14)	178
Clara-Jayne Wicks (12)	179
Isabel Turner (12)	180
Alisha Kilbey (11)	181
Harrison Springall (13)	182
Jessica Gilbert (13)	183
Sonnie Bishop (14)	184
Libby Bowyer (12)	185
Gemma Woods (12)	186
Eden Florence Gediking (12)	187
Beth Stinson (13)	188
Jessica Thomas (15)	189
Fletcher Henry Walls (12)	190
Zac Liley (15)	191
Joshua Clemence (11)	192
Holly Jayne Van Blerk (13)	193
Mollie Deanna Mitchell (12)	194
Franklin James Farren (13)	195
Brooke Taylor Powell (11)	196
Melissa Argent (12)	197
Blue French (11)	198
Alexia Mullane (12)	199
Ewan Thomson (14)	200
Finlay Fox (11)	201
Ashden Lyons (12)	202
Chloe Carter (14)	203
Samuel Pointer (11)	204
Tom Robb (11)	205
Rebecca Anne Bloomfield (11)	206
Yasmin Leah Hague (13)	207
Lewis Gardiner (11)	208
James Richardson (14)	209
Lewis Dean (12)	210
Mia Staples (12)	211
Noah Bradnock (13)	212
Dylan Brown (12)	213
Evangeline Forman (11)	214
Ted Hatcher (12)	215
Joe Maurins (12)	216

THE POEMS

The Lion At The Zoo's Point Of View

How dare you stand there and stare at me through the glass,
Watching me go about my daily business,
As I stand and swish my hair, you just glare,
Not thinking how rude this is to me.
You humans think I adore my life,
But no, this place is just my prison.
I never get a minute to myself,
You love to paparazzi me, using me as a backdrop for selfies,
Like they would go out of fashion.
You just don't understand how annoying you can be,
How am I supposed to make memories, here, when I'm stuck in this cage?
If I could talk, I would say
You're a foul species, a selfish species, one that only thinks about themselves.
I hate this place, I wish I could be free,
But no, you brought me here, for your amusement.
You have had your fun, now set me free,
So I can live my life.
No longer would I be afraid and have to waste my time pacing up and down this cage,
I'd finally have a life of my own,
My time has come, please just let me be free!

Elly-May Parsons (12)
Furness Academy, Barrow-In-Furness

A Balloon At A Birthday Party

As I sit here
Listening to children shout and cheer
Watching them dance, jump and run
Whilst all having fun

A single blue balloon
Which reminds me of the moon.
In a sea of balloons of all different colours
The blue balloon stands out more than the others.

The kids are all unaware
As I sit and stare
At this blue balloon
Dancing to the music, seemingly in tune.

The children are quiet
Now food is arriving and they all know
It's nearly time for birthday cake
With excitement, they all shake.

Then, suddenly, a loud pop!
The blue balloon had reached the top.
It caught the lights, now down it falls
The children carry on, take no notice at all.

It's home time now, time to go.
The children, all happy, faces aglow.
The birthday girl, with her birthday gifts
Is sad because her biggest wish

Was the blue balloon, that is no more
Now she realises, it's on the floor.
She cries and weeps, she wants it back
Dad saves the day, he has a full, new pack.

Niamh Marr (13)
Furness Academy, Barrow-In-Furness

Hell

Everything's falling apart.
Sirens and planes muffle our hearing
of the bombs hitting us on Earth,
as the rain falls and people run.
I stand to watch, hoping I will be able to witness the sweet
sorrow of our dear city falling apart,
why I want to watch, I don't know.
It's just something about the way I stand,
invisible to the world.

Not a word, scream or look was thrown my way.
The broken glass and shattered hearts will remain on jet-black, ash-covered streets.
As mornin' began to break through,
a dull light shone in the war zone.

Lifeless bodies lay mute, under the weight of other innocent objects,
like an open secret,
the city that once sat in glory, sits in vain.
Gone,
all gone!
No one in sight!
Memories of the past jump around,
I imagine a life without evil.
But what is evil?

It hides in the most well-seeming forms,
like an angel sent from heaven.

But really it's a demon sent from hell.

Lydia-Hope Hill (15)
Furness Academy, Barrow-In-Furness

Mindblown

I'm going to watch Aladdin,
With my popcorn friends,
I hope I don't get eaten
Before the movie ends.

This cardboard box is home for now,
I'm sitting at the top,
I used to be a kernel,
But then my head went *pop!*

We're all sweet and salty,
Me and all my mates,
We're the pricey snack of choice,
When going on a date.

This is my friend Colin,
Best pals since we were seeds,
This hand keeps making grabs for us,
So scared we nearly screamed.

Oh no! Here comes the hand again,
He's taking all my friends,
If he gets his hands on me,
I'm sure it'll be the end.

He took hold of me gently,
And put me in his mouth,
Then his teeth went chew, chew, chew,
And I was swallowed south.

I'm back again with all my friends,
We don't know what to do,
They all miss being popcorn,
I know that I do too.

Amelia Leach (12)
Furness Academy, Barrow-In-Furness

Spiders

When someone says, imagine,
you think of happy things.
Like flowers, stories, love, friends,
Queens and kings.

Now, what you don't think of are big, innocent spiders,
but what if I asked,
how would you feel if those small spiders were ginormous biters?

You might laugh,
it couldn't happen.
Giant spiders don't exist.
Except in your imagination.

But my friend knows they are real.

She thought it was cool to stomp on spiders,
pulling legs off in the park.
Until, one night, she fell asleep,
and heard them coming through the dark.

Enormous spiders using crutches,
filled her mind and filled her room.
Wrapped her quickly like a mummy,
sucked her blood and sang a tune -

We are spiders.
We play nice,
spinning beauty,
catching dew,
until you harm our spider sisters,
then we have to come for you!

Shana McMullan (13)
Furness Academy, Barrow-In-Furness

The Amazon

I am a chimpanzee,
I like to swing from tree to tree,
I live in the Amazon with my family,
But soon I will not.
All I can hear is the sound of trees being chopped,
And the cry of the animals being separated from their families.

I am a jaguar,
I like to chase my prey,
I live in the Amazon with my family,
But soon I will not.
I am not oblivious to the blazes,
My family were killed by the fires,
Now I am lonesome and sad,
And spent my days wandering alone.

I am a tapir,
I like to laze in waters,
I live in the rainforest with my family,
But soon I will not.
I miss the good old days with my friends,
But now they are gone,
The poachers came and they still do,
So I hide away with my family every time they do.

We are the endangered species of the Amazon,
And we are coming to you today
To say, please help to save us.

Ella Benson (12)
Furness Academy, Barrow-In-Furness

The Beach

The beach lies scattered with empty shells,
The rock pools are giving off pungent smells.
Worms are buried in the sand,
While crabs are scuttling across the land.
Soon the sea will head to shore,
And all these things we'll see no more.
Waves will lap across the sand,
And stop at the edge of the Earth's dry land.
The world below will come alive,
Where all marine life live and thrive.
Gannets hunt among the waves,
Looking for fish delicacies that they crave.
Fishermen set up to catch a prize,
Scores of fish they'll catch alive.
Soon the tide will turn away,
Just as it does twice every day.
Once the sea has left the shore,
All will be as it was before.
The sand will glisten in the sun,
While sea creatures hide or run.
The beach is now an empty floor,
Waiting for the sea to return once more.

Angel Joanna Beckman (11)
Furness Academy, Barrow-In-Furness

The Poster

All day, every day,
Floods of children coming into the classroom.
Yet I'm still here, twenty-four hours of the day.
Not one look at me, lonely,
Dead inside as I am blanked all day, every day.
And then it happened, they pointed at me,
Referred to me as useful and helpful.
A spark lit inside me, I lit up with excitement,
Feeling like I am being used and I have a meaning.

Then it happened again, here I am, all day every day,
Feeling lonely and not have any meaning and no one to turn to.
Sitting here doing nothing, words written on my face,
I don't know what they say, but I am not helpful, so they can't be good.
What is my meaning in this room? What do I do but sit here and do nothing?
Why am I here if I can't do anything good?
I can't do anything.

Michael Milby (13)
Furness Academy, Barrow-In-Furness

The Perfect Gift

I waited patiently in a box,
waiting for a big surprise.
I heard unknown, happy voices.
They opened me up and hugged me,
I ran around and licked everyone.

A few years later,
they are petting me again,
I couldn't wait to go outside,
run around and play.
My legs are aching, my eyes close,
I wake up in a bright room,
talking voices, seeming sad.

Next, I see my owners cry.
They watch me, hug and kiss me
and say goodbye, as the keyboard types.
I am in pain but try to get up,
some leave but some stay.
They stroke me and sob silently.

I know I have to go,
but I don't like the pain,
so let me be in peace,
I'll watch you live happily.

But now
I have to let go...

I feel my pain go and my eyes close.

Ashlee Dickinson (13)
Furness Academy, Barrow-In-Furness

Pencil

Used without consent,
My rights, the rules, all bent.
I have no friends in that case,
They hurt me with how they embrace.
All my friends bent and snapped,
They use us for our lead and that's a fact.
Sometimes we snap, that's how it is,
But does that let them treat us like this?
They scrape at our skin, agonising pain,
The more they use us, the more we drain.

We are rubber-headed, wood created,
But they treat us like we are left for dead, or cremated.
They harass us, leave us in tears,
I don't get it, you wouldn't torture your peers.
Leave us alone, let us be,
Or you'll be next, just wait and see.
You've heard my complaints, make a decision,
Correct your ways or see what we envision.

Daniel Nicholson (12)
Furness Academy, Barrow-In-Furness

A Game Of Football

In summer's warmth or winter's chill,
The beautiful game is full of thrills,
Wearing shin pads and boots on their feet,
We would be gutted if this ends in defeat.

Thousands of fans soon to arrive,
Some have walked, some drive,
Coloured scarves and football tops,
Most have got their club's props.

The game now starts, the whistle blows,
All this tension from the word 'go',
Shooting and passing, rival fans harassing,
The players don't care, they are now out-classing.

Here they come, *ping, ping, ping*
We are cheering, some fans sing,
The ball gets struck into the back of the net,
The rival fans are now upset, this is certainly a day to forget.

Nathan Boyes (13)
Furness Academy, Barrow-In-Furness

Michael Jackson

We are the world, we are the children.
Even though I made songs for you,
gave to charities and helped dying children with food,
you don't believe the one you sued.

I did no wrong and stayed in the lights,
but I did not stand up for my rights.

I died exhausted,
why can't you see?
Wrapped with the pain and the misery.

We are the world, we are the children.
'Leave Me Alone', hear that song and see
because right now, I am free!

We are all the world, we are all the children,
so I made this poem for you.
What can I do?
I'm gone now.
But do not blame yourself,
as time might see me done,
as not everything in this world can be undone.

Kayley Blezard (11)
Furness Academy, Barrow-In-Furness

Aircraft In The High Sky

Landing wheels up and we're off,
people walking up and down my belly.
An old man awaits his cup of tea as he coughs,
flight crew walking up and down my belly, serving young
babies jelly.

Start off in a cold country,
end up in a warm one.
I feel like every day I am doing a cross-country,
I feel like I should just give up and do none.

Bags, bags, bags,
I am constantly filled with bags!
Passing all kinds of different flags,
and I am always being nagged.

But I think I make a friend,
but they always leave after two hours, that's what they all
do.
But it doesn't bother me, all I do is blend
into the sky, blue.

Harry McMurdo (13)
Furness Academy, Barrow-In-Furness

I Wonder

I sit in my chair
and glance outside
the room is as noisy as a dozen drums.
People coming in and out of the room,
as noisy as a train station.
People prodding me,
left, right and centre.
And then... once they have had their little dig,
the blare seems to stop.
The room falls as quiet as an icy, tranquil lake.

But I know,
sometime later they won't be able to resist
my beautiful smile.
Their hands all over me.
Huge hands overshadowing my tiny face,
whispers about me.

The people think they're just being sweet
but they don't feel my pain.
If they don't have a good nosey
at me, then they feel incomplete.

Holly Warbrick (13)
Furness Academy, Barrow-In-Furness

Lonely As My Shadow

As lonely as my shadow,
and yes, I'm talking about me,
a friendly, harmless ghost,
who loves a cup of tea.

Children don't like me,
they say I look scary,
but it's not as if they'll turn around
and see a magic fairy.

All I want is to have a friend
and play with them at school.
They would love me like they love their mum
and treat me like a special jewel.

I think if I wasn't scary,
and they would understand,
my life would be so much brighter,
living here on land.

So, if you see a ghost,
pop and say hello,
don't make them feel like I do,
as lonely as my shadow.

Violet Mae Bland (11)
Furness Academy, Barrow-In-Furness

Tragedy

I am lonely, depressed,
Every now and then I have nightmares,
I am trapped, trapped never to be free,
A plain, smooth, stripped hand reached for me,
My hat came off,
Falling, falling until the end,
I glanced over a plain sky-white piece of paper,
Letters were cloned,
Some weren't right,
Then to be gone,
Ink ran down my cheek,
Begging to be let go,
Words were trapped, trapped in this chamber door,
I could not take much more,
Begging, shouting, howling to be let go,
Dreaming every lost soul to be let free,
Finally, I could be what I wanted to be,
Free,
But never to be seen once more.

Christos Smargiannakis (12)
Furness Academy, Barrow-In-Furness

I'd Like To Be A Car

I look up and all I see is stars and darkness
from the glass roof above me.
I see myself
all glistening and clean.
I want to be awoken, when will it be?
I hear something different to what I do usually,
the thing that warms me.
Two seconds later, I start to growl and rumble.
I suddenly feel so powerful.
The thing screams in happiness,
starts to press something,
I suddenly feel compelled to growl again.
I backfire, then I see sparks from a wire.
I do what no car would desire -
I drive without order.
The garage door flies open,
I go full pace,
no time to save.

Theo Christopher Powell (13)
Furness Academy, Barrow-In-Furness

Pencil Case Poem

I'm full of handy tools
that you use for school.
I sit for twenty-four hours, on my base,
until someone decides to pick up my case.
As the pencil escapes the case,
I can never find the trace.
If you draw too dark,
I will never rub out the mark.
Your underlining is way cooler
when you use a ruler.
Without a doubt,
I will soon be worn out.
If you forget me,
your bag will feel empty.
I've got rubbers and rulers,
not like all those other losers.
You can get me in any colour you desire,
but beware, the price might get higher.

Lacey Smith (13)
Furness Academy, Barrow-In-Furness

My Dead Heroic Dog

I'm Max,
I'm black
and white.
I have brown eyes
and I'm a medium size,
but my life is hard.
I'm my owner's emotional support animal
because of bullies.
My owner used to come home
and ball her eyes out,
while
cuddling me.
She used to talk to me
but I can't hear very well,
because I'm deaf in one ear and not in the other,
and I'm blind in one eye and not in the other.

I was twelve
so I was old and ill,
my owners didn't know about it.
Goodbye Brooke...

Brooke Smith-Hadwick (13)
Furness Academy, Barrow-In-Furness

My Week

On Monday, I feel sad
because I have to go to school.

On Tuesday, I feel tired
because I had a long day yesterday.

On Wednesday, I was starting to get excited
because it is nearly the weekend.

On Thursday, I'm happy
because it is two more days 'til the weekend.

On Friday, I'm happy
because I'm having chips for dinner.

On Saturday, I'm excited
because it is the weekend.

On Sunday, I became sad again
because it is the end of the weekend and I have to go to school tomorrow.

Lexi-Mia Grove (12)
Furness Academy, Barrow-In-Furness

Cellphones

Running,
Can't stop, must be fast,
Slow down a bit and you are last.
Bullying and heinous crimes,
People blame us but not who's behind,
People read us but not between the lines.
People never ask if we are fine,
Use us without consent,
Yeah, we don't mind.
Insults flying from left to right,
We try to stop you,
But you carry on and fight.
We help you out, that's what we strive,
Friends don't let friends
Text and drive.
So many mistakes made in life,
Yet many don't give high-fives.

Seth Mills (12)
Furness Academy, Barrow-In-Furness

I'd Love To Be A Tree

I'd love to be a tree,
to see all the sights,
as funny as it can be,
to see the little children all happy and riding bikes.

I'd love to be a tree,
to sit on top of a hill,
to do nothing all day,
relax, watch the world go by and chill.

I'd love to be a tree,
a large one perhaps,
to doze around all day,
and chat with my old, large chaps.

I'd love to be a tree
and not make a scene,
'cause I know that, one day,
I'd be a great table for the Queen.

Freddie Lawton (13)
Furness Academy, Barrow-In-Furness

The Pencil

Scratch! Creak!
Went my head as it started to shrink.
Blink, blink,
my eyes went as they started to shrink.
It's happened before, now it's happening again.
Why, oh why can paper kill me?
I try to hide in a pencil case,
I try to hide on the floor,
I can't stand this anymore!

People use my family a lot,
I've started to think they have lost the plot,
they have started to use us to make dots!
I've had enough!

She's coming with a new pack?

Mabel Vernon Charles (11)
Furness Academy, Barrow-In-Furness

Dog's Life

I can remember as a pup,
I was drinking out of a cup
I went through life having fun,
Eating a bun.

One day,
In May,
I fell ill,
Very ill.

I was weak,
My owner cuddled me tight,
Like it was going to be all right,
But I was scared.

One day,
My time had come,
I had to go,
I was no longer in pain,
I will miss you though.

I completed the family,
Even though it was all crazy,
I was once eleven,
And now I'm in heaven.

Ruby Palmer (14)
Furness Academy, Barrow-In-Furness

Poisonous Apple

I took the apple from the little lady,
She told me to eat it,
It was shiny, red,
I took a bite and...
Bang! I fell on the floor.
I was there for quite a long time,
'Til a Prince came and woke me up,
With true love's kiss.

Demi Rawlinson (13)
Furness Academy, Barrow-In-Furness

The Holder Of The Soul

Slithery, scaly old snake,
surely this must be a mistake.
They say that it is a curse that can't be broken, like a cuff,
but I am not a fool because I know this is a bluff.
I belong to the one who shall not be named,
and he will be the one who is tamed.
He controls me,
just so he can kill thee.
When I hear a call,
he makes me kill all.
One quick bite,
it will be a delight.
To him, I shine,
therefore he will dine.

Keiron Egerton (13)
Furness Academy, Barrow-In-Furness

Football Net

I want to see some action today.
Let it in.
My life is so boring,
I hate pre-season because I am not seeing any action.

I love it when Lionel Messi scores
an absolute screamer
because he makes it seem effortless.
Neymar, with his rainbow flick, taking players on
then finishing it,
top bins in,
amazing.

I only get ninety minutes of action a week,
then, after that, I don't get to see any more.

Bailey McLaughlin (13)
Furness Academy, Barrow-In-Furness

My Poem

Match day.
I can feel the excitement in the atmosphere
I hear the crowd cheering
then I was lifted from the podium
and placed on the centre spot.
The crowd goes silent,
the referee blows his whistle.
I am no longer motionless
as I surge through the air.
A half is almost gone but
in that moment
Messi strikes and
I go soaring into the top right corner of the net.
1-0
2-0
3-0
Lionel Messi scores a hat-trick.

Jack O'Neill (13)
Furness Academy, Barrow-In-Furness

Is It True Love?

Love is a word,
but a drug we depend on.
Love can hurt if we use it too much.

Hate is a word,
but a medicine we can depend on.
Hate can heal if we use it right,
but can hurt if we use it wrong.

Hate and love are words
that can hurt just as much as each other can.

Hate and love are two powerful words
stronger than each other.
But, what's not a word
that is affected by all words?

A family.

Steph Carter (14)
Furness Academy, Barrow-In-Furness

In The Ocean

In the ocean, the plastic is deadly,
But it is getting worse, fast and steadily.
Plastic bags and plastic bottles for drinks,
But plastic is causing our deaths, so stop and think!

It's our world, you need to care,
It's the only one we have and we have to share.

Save us from plastic in the sea,
Let's take action now, I think you will agree.
Save our seas before it's too late,
Otherwise, I will lose another mate.

Macy McArthur (11)
Furness Academy, Barrow-In-Furness

Endangered

As I watch the plastic being left, helplessly,
carelessly on the sand beach,
I remember how the sea used to be.
Crystal-blue waves diving over my head,
pulsing into the ocean.
Coral reefs full to the brim,
bursting with colour,
we all lived happily then.

But now, dark grey waves pounding through the ocean,
coral reefs dead and grey in colour.
We all live unhappily,
an endangered species soon gone.

Amelia Massey Holmes (11)
Furness Academy, Barrow-In-Furness

The Mighty Anfield

The mighty Anfield is our home
and we all sing
'You Will Never Walk Alone'.
Our leader is Mr Jurgen Klopp.
The Scousers love him,
especially the Kop.
We are the mighty reds,
we play Friday, Saturday, Sunday nights.
As we watch the strong eleven,
they never walk alone, so we sing.
When he left we found it hard,
Steven Gerrard.
The glory will come back
there is no rush.

Daniel Keay (12)
Furness Academy, Barrow-In-Furness

Black Roses

The roses are black and dark,
My hair waves with blonde marks,
I want to follow the lines,
But all I can do is lie,
The roses fill the yard,
Love fills my big, warm heart,
My bright blue eyes shine,
With the tree's twine,
Each rose is full of mystery,
With a different history,
I want more,
But I always ignore,
The black roses are full of wonder,
But there's always thunder.

Jamie-Leigh Thorley (12)
Furness Academy, Barrow-In-Furness

Old

The walls crack and chip around me,
The paint peels from its home,
An old radio sits on a table nearby,
A relic of a time I could never be part of.

When my father dies, I will be the only one who looks like him,
I'll decay and become a relic, I'll be just like my father,
I'll be like that radio, the walls and paint,
I'll be a drum made of skin, echoing my lost generation.

Charlie Bo Caine (12)
Furness Academy, Barrow-In-Furness

A Fishing Poem

Fishing is a worldwide sport,
How many fish have you caught?
Cast your rod into the water,
When you reel it in, you shout "I caught her!"

Fish are fast, slimy and scaly,
Fishermen that are good catch daily.
Angler fish, teeth like needles,
This fish is big enough to feed us.

One fish, one hook,
One rod and one fisherman can change the world!

Charlie Morgan (12)
Furness Academy, Barrow-In-Furness

A Pen

People chew on me when they think,
Then throw me away when I run out of ink.

I sit around in Keira's pencil case,
When her sister falls asleep, we draw on her face.

It's hard work being little old me,
Everyone takes me for granted, you see.

I get chewed and stood on and kicked and tossed,
And everyone blames each other when I get lost.

Keira Shand-Lupton (13)
Furness Academy, Barrow-In-Furness

The Car

As I wake up, my engine roars,
My lights turn on, you open my doors,
The wheels start to spin,
I'm in for the win.

He fills my tank,
And then my heart sank, as I nearly crashed,
In the final dash,
Over the finish line.

My tyres are burning,
From all of the turning,
I'm ready for a wash,
After I collect all of the dosh.

Jack Whittall (13)
Furness Academy, Barrow-In-Furness

Boris Johnson's Hairbrush

Sat lonely on the dustiest shelf in the house,
Sits a sparkly, bright pink hair brush.
I have only been used once or twice.
I have been sat here for months,
Just waiting to be used,
I'm surprised I don't have dust disease by now.
Every time he walks past, with his cup of tea in his Beyoncé cup,
My face lights up with hope,
But no!

Tia Mullen (11)
Furness Academy, Barrow-In-Furness

All The People In Life

If you think laughing at someone is cool,
Think again, because it is probably cruel.
But in your friends, you see a light,
They are the real ones to keep in life.
Being present, you should be nice,
Because there is no reason to start a fight.
Because becoming a liar will soon backfire.
So realise, in life,
You'll always have to be nice.

Nikita Wilding (12)
Furness Academy, Barrow-In-Furness

The Unwanted One

Shoved in a corner,
Always ignored,
A lonely book is worthless to the core.
Looking for an owner,
One never seems to come,
It sits in sadness,
Raging with madness.
Why should this book have to wait?
Maybe a child may just pick it up one day.
In the shadows of the popular books,
This book just never gets a look.

Lauren Hewson (12)
Furness Academy, Barrow-In-Furness

The Bully

Just because you're small and he's tall,
doesn't mean he's above us all.

Just because he calls you 'gay'
doesn't mean you run away.

Get out of bed, take off the mask.
Even though it's a massive task.

Stand up to the bully, look at the eyes.
Don't be scared, don't be shy...
because I am the bully.

Maddie Shepherd (12)
Furness Academy, Barrow-In-Furness

What Is It In The Sewer?

What is that I hear?
A sewer full of fear.
I kneel near the drain,
And hear a scream of pain,
I shout "Hello!"
And I hear the echo below.
I stick my hand in,
To feel something within.
A clown I see,
Jumping up with glee.
Saying, "You'll float too."
What on earth should I do?

Zachary James Downing (12)
Furness Academy, Barrow-In-Furness

Trees

Autumn trees,
Leaves fall in the breeze,
Colours so beautiful I almost fall to my knees.
Chilly, cold, I hope I don't sneeze.
Autumn trees, I plead you don't freeze,
Surrounded by colour, you certainly do please.
Oh, autumn trees, I hope you never disease,
You will live on forever,
That is what I believe.

Emily Miller (12)
Furness Academy, Barrow-In-Furness

Mirror

A mirror is like a portal,
It shows you the truth.
But that's not how you see it
When you look at yourself in a mirror,
You see someone completely different,
As if all your bad features are more prominent,
Like a funhouse.
A mirror will never tell the truth,
No matter how long you stare.

Khian Joseph Phizacklea Powell (13)
Furness Academy, Barrow-In-Furness

The Days Of The Week

Monday, I feel like I'm down in the dumps.
Tuesday still has lots of bumps.
Wednesday I am halfway through the week.
Thursday, the weekend is beginning to peek.
Friday is pie day, one more day to go.
Saturday - it's the weekend! I feel a glow.
Sunday means it's nearly Monday.

Ella Moon (12)
Furness Academy, Barrow-In-Furness

Inking For You

Every day I work for them,
yet they take me apart,
look at my insides,
bite my head.
I do wish that they would notice my hard work.

Finlay Crompton (12)
Furness Academy, Barrow-In-Furness

A Daily Life Of A Soldier (My Dad)

I begin my journey home,
but I feel so alone.
As I come home from Afghanistan,
all I can think about is going to Pakistan.
Because I am in the military,
sometimes, my life is solitary.

Joshua Brown (12)
Furness Academy, Barrow-In-Furness

The World's Gone Mad

What's crazy or mad?
What's demented or absurd?
What's mad to you?

I'll tell you,
It's you and I,
And my mother, your mother,
My father, your father.

It's us,
All of us,
Every single one.

Why?
Why say such a thing?
Why insult me like that?
I often ask myself the same thing.

Why do we omit the most significant,
The most daunting of news, facts,
Truth?

Why do we hide away from reality?
Yet never escape society,
The media.

Why do we bypass the truth?
The horrifying, deathly truth,

Our intentions should be to stay alive,
To live.

But what do we spend our lives doing?
Speaking of people with too much money to handle,
Of what someone is wearing,
Of our appearances,
Of how we felt when we were told no.

Why do we choose not to use our voices when we need them?
Or when we could be saving someone?

Why do we masquerade ourselves as perfect,
As happy,
Or sad?

Why do we not use social media,
Or our voices,
Or our followers?

When we find out that we have twelve years to save the planet,
Or that, in order for you to turn on the mobile phone you probably use for hours daily,
Someone risked their life atop baneful peaks, mining for the materials,
Or that 30,000 children died today due to lack of clean drinking water.
Were you aware of this?

Or were you too busy thinking of other things,
More important things,
Like politics,
And how many followers you have,
Or if the WiFi is working?

There is only one reason we are like this,
We've simply gone mad.

Aimee Caulkin (13)
Handsworth Wood Girls' Academy, Birmingham

The Anti-Bullying Team

Listen up, you bullies, we are the anti-bullying team,
we're here to let you know you can't destroy our self-esteem.
Together we are stronger, you will never make us break,
we really don't resent, it's pity that we take.
Listen up, you bullies, and it's time to listen well,
until this moment you have put us through hell,
you've punched us and you kicked us and pushed us to the floor.
Listen up, you bullies, we're the anti-bullying pro's,
we'll rise above the riot as we stand up on our toes.
Combining all our forces, we stand tall,
the anti-bullying team will make you bullies feel so small.

Suliana Bahta (11)
Handsworth Wood Girls' Academy, Birmingham

Started From Block Number One

I spawn into the world, dreaming of how it would end.
"Right," I sighed, as I started to wander to the tree,
"Aah!" I screamed, but actually it was a buzzing bee.
I started to walk further into the sunset,
But suddenly, I realised that I had no cosy bed!
"Oh gosh, there's no wool or sheep nearby," I said.
"I better take shelter before all the googlies come out."
And so I did, but I doubt I'd stay alive.

The next morning came, I decided to find a cave,
So I got my pickaxe and torches and made my way.
I found coal, iron, lapis, and some gold,
However, I wasn't looking for that.
I felt quite bold, and decided to jump over lava too,
Are those diamonds? The ore I've been searching for?
I was screaming with joy, they were so neon blue!
Oh, I wish I could search for even more.

A few weeks later, I had everything I needed,
From armour to magical, healing potions.
There I was, fighting the deadly Ender dragon,
I'd slay a wacky wither and a screeching ghast,
But I have never slain something this powerful before.
Slash! Plash! Whoosh! Bam!
I got my glass bottle and caught the dragon's pink breath,
One more stab with my shiny, diamond sword,
Boom! It was gone and the experience was everywhere.

There it was, the dragon egg... that treasure is so rare!
My favourite game completed, and I didn't know what to do,
I finished the game, finally, it was done,
But it all started from block number one.

Andreja Elijosiute
Handsworth Wood Girls' Academy, Birmingham

Undying Love

Trapped in a figment of my imagination,
Staring into the precious blue gems of my creation.
My dazzling hallucination.
A kaleidoscope of emotions locked within,
As you reach to stroke my fragile chin.
A cold sensation creeping up my spine,
Telling them, 'I'm just fine',
You and I will last forever,
Dancing in my memories, following me wherever.
Trapped for eternity near your side,
Like Jekyll and Hyde.
Together we are one,
Basking beside you in the glow of the midnight sun.
His ghastly pale face hovering amongst the mist,
His ice-cold skin grabbed my wrist.
His blue eyes searing into my numb soul,
Echoing into the hollowness of the heart you stole.
Floating elegantly in my mind,
Memories of me, the girl you left behind.
Your pale memories swooping before my eyes in disbelief,
Surrounded by condolences and drowning in grief.
You are the fleshless reminder of my past,
And our love for each other was bound to last.
The loss of you was one so deep,
I must leave you to your beautiful heartbreaking sleep.
Our love goes beyond the grave,

But alas, it is my soul I shall save.
Your love will last with me 'til the end of time,
I bid you farewell, one last time.
I must let you go,
But you will forever be my beau.

Isma Rahiem (14)
Handsworth Wood Girls' Academy, Birmingham

Through Their Eyes

A hungry child,
devoid of hope,
this world has robbed all of their joy.
Every waking moment
feels like another year in hell,
but we will never see
through their eyes.
We watch the news,
we sigh and cry,
our sentiments do not fill that child,
sharing posts on your social media
or complaining at night
will do nothing for that child.
We will never feel
the pain in their lives.

An abused child,
beaten every night,
they have never felt the love of a mother
or the joy of a father.
The rotting feeling
that no one will ever care.
We will never see
through their eyes.
We see the shelters
filled with broken souls,
we shy away from donating a few pounds,

our pity will not save that child.
We will never feel
the emptiness in their soul

The outcast child,
standing alone at school,
three-inch scars decorate their arms,
but we will never see
through their eyes.
We put up mental health posters,
we insist that they are not alone,
every day a new social media post.
But we will never feel the gaping hole of loneliness
in their heart,
we will never feel
what it is like
to hate the body you were born into.
We will never see
through their eyes
or feel the pain in their body.

So we must act,
or they will all be gone.
Be kind to your friends,
do the work to help those children,
do not sit idly by
while the child population of our world
slowly dies.

Lael Lopez (17)
Interhigh School, Crickhowell

The Way The World Is Run

Life is hard,
A sentence we hear nearly every day,
But yet other people still try and make life harder.
People judge,
They judge hard,
They judge you for what you wear,
How you speak,
Your face,
Anything.
People think it's okay,
People think it's okay to judge others,
For who they are,
For what they believe,
For what they think.
Why do people want us to be the same?
We're all different,
You can't change that,
However hard you try.
It doesn't matter if you're
Black or white,
Gay or straight,
Blonde or brunette,
Everyone deserves to be themselves.
The world is more experienced,
Yet society still judges.
When will people learn that it's not okay?

When will people realise that we're all humans?
When will people realise that we have feelings?
When will people learn that you can treat people nicely?
The end of the world,
Won't be because of a nuclear bomb,
It will be people's words.
It will be people's words that ruin the world.
Words are the most powerful things,
They influence you,
The way you see things,
The way the world is run.

Katie Riley (13)
Interhigh School, Crickhowell

Lonely

Why does loneliness come in the dark night?
When everybody is in sleepy starlight,
I am awake, in my thoughts,
also, deep asleep,
my head goes trembling, I cannot breathe.
Then I awake in the deep, blue sea.
For there, loneliness grants me
with its daring and mysterious smile.
For we put hand in hand,
and dance together for a while.
It wraps me tight in its comforting restraint.
As I drift away, I gain my consciousness.
For I know our dance is over, and dawn is here.
I remember that being with loneliness is quite comforting,
for it understands.
But I know what loneliness does.
When you think of it as a friend,
going to it for warmth and peacefulness,
giving it complete trust.
When it has gained it,
in a blink of an eye, it gets you and swallows you whole.
For loneliness is a hunter and you are the prey.

Fiza Iqbal (17)
Interhigh School, Crickhowell

Traffic Warden

As I rip the ticket off the book,
Some passers-by give me a dirty look -
I sigh and stick the ticket to the windscreen,
It's not me, I'm not mean.

I just don't know what to say,
I do this job every day.
And in my time, I've seen some crazily parked cars -
I wonder if these people have come from Mars.

Do you want to know the worst parking crime?
The most unworthy of my time.
Definitely, the most deserving of a fine,
It's parking on a double red line.

My job here is finally done,
Now it's time to have some fun.
At my cosy, beautiful home,
To the kitchen where I can freely roam.

But wait what's that on my windscreen,
A yellow ticket with the number eighteen.
Oh my goodness, it can't be,
Not a parking ticket for me!

Sara Mughal (12)
Interhigh School, Crickhowell

Home-Icide*

One of these days you'll need me but I won't be there,
I would've already melted away in despair.
One of these days you won't have a protector,
Your sun heating you up - if only there was a way to deflect her...

One of these days your ways will wash upon you,
Patiently, I will swish and swash; then come crashing down on you.
One of these days they will blame you, maleficent malefactors,
Generations to come labelling you the 'extreme extractors'.

One of these days you'll drown in my ice-cold blood,
Desperately trying not to choke on the fact that you could've nipped this all in the bud.

*The killing of a habitat by its inhabitants

Yusuf Naveed Khan (15)
Interhigh School, Crickhowell

Through Their Eyes

Yesterday, your beauty enriched the ocean,
We lost ourselves in a rainbow of delight.
For humans, you were a magical potion,
So much to see, so much that was right.
Today, the sea is warming,
All is not what it used to be.
Our coral home, with creatures swarming.
What is happening to our lively sea?
Tomorrow the water will overheat,
The reefs of the world will die.
No longer will our brave hearts beat,
The people of the world will sigh.
If you could see the reefs, through our eyes,
You would change your ways, becoming wise.

Yashodah Moodley (12)
Interhigh School, Crickhowell

Who Will Win?

Who will win? Nobody knows,
There are so many of us that we have friends and foes,
It would be awfully hard to choose just one,
But there's a decision to be made and it must be done.

How about Mandarin? I'm the best,
Forever in every single fest',
I am world known,
There's no one better than me 'cause I'm as strong as bone.

You're a great big show-off that's what you are,
Everybody knows English is the star,
I am so complicated, so I need a whole subject too,
I am sure that I am way better than you.

Show-off you say? How about yourself?
I own so many books they could fill billions of shelves,
Over one billion people speak me in China alone,
My language is more valuable than a gemstone.

Stop arguing, this is getting us nowhere,
But since we're on this topic, I'd suggest you beware,
Twenty-one countries have Spanish as their official dialect,
My words are built carefully, like an architect.

How about Arabic?
People find me addictive,
I am the language of the Muslim's holy book,
I am used in recipes which are delicious to cook.

How about me - Hindustani? I'm a mix of a religion and a country,
Hindu and Pakistani,
English has borrowed some of my vocabulary,
You've used bangles, shampoo and chutney.

It's true, I am sewn using various dialects,
But English is unique in other aspects,
I am the official language of the air,
This proves that I am truly rare.

Arabic is clever and sophisticated,
The beauty of my language isn't exaggerated,
I flow when spoken and a beauty to behold,
I am used in quite a few households.

Many people speak my language all around
I was first used in Gaul, a wondrous town,
I believe I am one of the best,
And, for that reason, French is truly blessed.

Who shall we choose? All of us are great,
But there are many more languages, so we can't decide our fate,
Or maybe the world should stay the same,
Although this would be a bit of a shame.

Zahra Amjad (11)
Lady Aisha Academy, Barking

Alone

She sits there
Nothing to look forward to
Nothing to look back on
Here, with me
But not knowing she has company

She sits there
Alone
I wish I could reach out to her
But I can't
I'm just here

She sits there
Occasionally, tears streaming down her face
But I can't wipe them
I can't tell her it's okay
I'm just here

She sits there
Alone
Blinded from the light
Never going out
Afraid of the world
Afraid of the truth

She sits there
Everything leaning against me
But I can never hold her up

I can only support her with my arms
Never by words

She sits there
Alone
Her face in her hands
Sprawled across the floor
Wishing she was dead

She sits there
Sometimes staring right at me
But her mind is elsewhere
Lost in deep, deep thought

She sits there
Alone
Hiding in my corner
From nothing but fear
Her heart yearning for something good
But all it can feel is emptiness

She sits there
Hating every minute of her life
Regretting every breath she takes
Hoping for the sign that has never come

She sits there
Alone
All day
All night

Never saying a word
Never making a sound

She sits there
Her eyes empty and sad
A deep sea, unexplored
Lost in an eternal darkness

She sits there
Alone
Hands trembling
Reaching out for something
Untouched

She sits there
Slowly twisting it
The ancient feeling beneath her fingers

She sits there
Alone
Pulling at it
With all her strength

She sits there
Open the door to the world
Opening her mind to the truth
Letting her heart feel joy
And for the first time ever
Realising she's not alone anymore...

Ammarah Talati (12)
Lady Aisha Academy, Barking

Colour

Why are people so mean to me all the time?

They never say nice comments to me,
When I was on the body of Rosa Parks, sometime,
There were others who looked unlike me.
They are the ones with lighter skin,
They make me feel like my colour is a sin.

How everyone makes fun of me,
Ouch, it hurts when everyone is against me.
I stretch around everyone's bodies,
I stand still to the ground,
Eyes, nose, lips and ears are all a part of me.

Standing by the shore, I wait to visit the sea to become tanned,
Days later, people make fun of me, saying that I never tan.
Why do people make such a fuss about me?
They take me as if I am different to everyone else,
When I am just the same as you and them.

Faridah Kaniz Zaman (11)
Lady Aisha Academy, Barking

Morning Routine

Tweet, tweet
That's all we can say

Hungry as a bear
We all have a fear
"What if she forgets about us?"
I reassure them and say
"She will never forget us
She never will."

Tweet, tweet
That's all we can say

We hear one of the birds say
"Look, look, she is getting up."
We all watch her
Through her glasshouse
She opens her ocean-blue eyes

Tweet, tweet
That's all we can say

We see her bump her head
Then get up again
Running as fast as a cheetah
Looking for her shoes
That seems to have run away

Tweet, tweet
That's all we can say

Finding her lost shoes
Putting them on violently
She trips over her long laces

Tweet, tweet
That's all we can say

She slowly sits down on her chair
She has a fear that one day we might fly
Eating her food
She remembers us
And slowly scatters some breadcrumbs
As she hums the tune of our tweet.

Saniya Bint Ibrahim (12)
Lady Aisha Academy, Barking

Dollar Bill

There once was a dollar,
Whose name was Bill,
He spent his life in a supermarket till.

He met yens and euros,
Rupees and pounds,
Even a coin dug from underground.

Bill was happy,
Bill was fine,
Until he heard his cosy till chime.

Out came Bill,
He thought it was a curse!
And was drowned into the depths of the deep, dark purse.

He was driven away,
In the cold, he ached,
But still, he managed to stay awake.

There Bill lay,
In a woman's palm,
Pleading himself to remain truly calm.

He saw Carol credit card
Pushed into a gap,
This was only the beginning of a mishap!

He was shoved into a machine,
In he went!
Just then, he began to repent.

There they were,
A whole lot,
All of them being squished to the top.

Dollars and dollars!
Cents and dimes,
He thought he was dreaming a hundred times.

Bill loved it there,
He couldn't stop grinning!
He felt a new adventure beginning...

Bushra Mariam Zaheer (11)
Lady Aisha Academy, Barking

On The Streets

I live out on the streets,
In the cold and in the heat,
My neighbours are the rats and mice,
I can't afford a sack of rice.
I'm always there,
But you don't care,
That even in the cold and heat,
I live out on the streets.

I live out on the streets,
In the cold and in the heat,
You only give me dirty looks,
And somehow think that I'm the crook.
I find shelter where there's space,
In the dump, all over the place,
And even in the cold and heat,
I live out on the street.

I live out on the street,
In the cold and in the heat.
With your words, you give me kicks,
When really I just need some Vicks,
For my deadly, chesty cough,
But, you rich and selfish greedy toffs,

Don't exactly really care,
That even when the roads are bare,
In the cold and in the heat,
I still live on the street.

Maariya Islam (11)
Lady Aisha Academy, Barking

Spider-Man

A single bite, that's all it took,
to make the transformation begin,
and then it happened.
Now, all that's left, is a hero and a spider.
Hiding his identity, roaming New York city in blue and red,
saving the good citizen's life from the Green Goblin.
He is the undefeatable
Spider-Man!

But it's not all fun and games,
his mind aches with stress and pain,
too much pressure, he might faint.
He isn't just a person to rate.
His whole life, saving people,
what a hero!
Jumping wall to wall,
tired and stressed on the inside.
But, on the outside, you all know him as the amazing
Spider-Man!

Momina Khan (12)
Lady Aisha Academy, Barking

Terrorism

We shouldn't be mourning just for New Zealand
We should be mourning for the world
A world in which we talk about peace
A world in which we talk about unity

These monster-like people
Expect us to fall
Expect us to crumble
Expect us to shatter
But, in reality
It's the total opposite

We unite as powerful people
We help
We give
But we never surrender

Today, we march
Hand in hand
To tell you that your bombs
Your guns
Are not working

So, listen up
Stop what you're doing
Because it has no impact
In fact, it makes us stronger.

Alizay Shah (12)
Lady Aisha Academy, Barking

Friendship

To me, a six-letter word that has such a big meaning,
Has got me over you, leaning.
My friend is someone I turn to when my spirits need a lift,
My friend is someone I treasure, for friendship is a gift.
My friend is someone that shouts at me for no reason,
But talks nonsense in every season.
My friend is someone I can definitely trust forever,
No matter if you're apart or together.
My friend is like a lasting treasure,
For they can bring so much pleasure.
My friend is someone who fills my heart with beauty, joy and grace,
My friend makes the world I live in a better and happier place.

Zaina Ali (12)
Lady Aisha Academy, Barking

Sweet Forever Pet

There is something missing in my home,
I feel it day and night,
I know it will take time and strength,
Before things feel quite right.

But just for now, I need to mourn,
My heart - it needs to mend,
Though some may say "It is just a pet,"
I know I have lost a friend.

You have brought such laughter to my life,
And richness to my home...
A constant friend through joy or loss,
With gentle, loving ways.

Companion, pal and confidante,
A friend I won't forget,
You will live for always in my heart,
My sweet forever pet.

Zaynah Bint-Sheraz (11)
Lady Aisha Academy, Barking

O Prophet Muhammed (S.A.W.)

Better than you has never crossed my eyes,
and your presence in this life never dies.

You were the leader that no one could be,
no one can be the leader that you were, it's a guarantee.

You would accept everyone into Islam,
and would greet everyone with salaam.

Not once did you discriminate a man,
your mission was to bring the Quran.

You never acted higher than anyone,
and in most battles, you won.

You are the light brought forth to my eyes,
the radiant moon in the dark night sky.

Aisha Mohammed (12)
Lady Aisha Academy, Barking

Who Am I?

Help me!
As I sit in this cage,
That doesn't yet lock in my rage,
As time passes,
So do I,
My whole life is ruined,
Every breath I take,
Is every life I take.

Why do I kill?
That too gives me the chills,
I've turned into a monster,
Even I am scared of my face,
I hate myself.

Does it give me pleasure,
To take other people's treasure?
Is this too cruel?
I thought I was like my mother, who was pure,
Who am I?
Am I even human?
Help me!
Please!

Khadijah Begum (12)
Lady Aisha Academy, Barking

Funny Family

Family is important
important as love.
You should never give up on your family.
Follow your family
you will be jolly.
Listen to your family
you will be happy.
Respect your family
you will be jolly.
Always love for your family what you love for yourself.

Play with your family
you will be happy.
Pray with your family
you will be jolly.
Cherish them while
you have them...

When they are gone
it will not be the same.
Always take care
of your fun, funny family.

Ruqayyah Zahra Siddiq (11)
Lady Aisha Academy, Barking

Our Tremendous Tongues

We live in dark, moist caves,
Our home is a little bit sharp,
Like any other home, we can hurt ourselves.

We're amazing...

We can be multi-lingual,
Hello, Hola, Bonjour, Ciao...
Not impressed yet?

We can do gymnastics,
We can wave, roll, turn and flip.
Not impressed yet?

We're also the ones who give you
flavours to savour.

We're the ones with power,
We can lead you to your fate,
So choose your words carefully,
To the good or bad gate!

Laaibah Rashid (11)
Lady Aisha Academy, Barking

The King Of The Jungle

You better not mess with me,
For I am the king,
The King of the jungle,
Yes, I am,
I am the one and only Lion King.

Yes, that's right, the Lion King,
So tremble in fear for I am the Lion King,
If I lay eyes on you when I'm hungry,
Then you better watch out.

Because once you've been targeted,
Then there's no escape,
I'm as strong as a bear,
I'm as sly as a snake,
And as smart as an elephant.

So just give up,
Because if you're my prey,
There's no escape.

Hawa Haydari (11)
Lady Aisha Academy, Barking

Grumpy Life

I go around the world,
with my smile upside down.
The sun sees me when I'm wandering around.
The wind howls, my hair flows,
why does life have to be so bad?

I lived in war, Egypt and more,
I was alive for many years
and no one noticed where I've gone.
Why does life have to be so sad?

But everything changed,
my heart and my pain,
Finally, someone bought me
from the store.
Now I can sleep
on the floor.
Life isn't so bad
as a grumpy cat.

Yasmin Abdul-Ghani (11)
Lady Aisha Academy, Barking

Social Media

I'm tired of being used,
My brain is going to fuse,
Everyone always tapping me,
Oh, what to do?

I'm tired of being used,
So many new posts,
Only when I die,
But what good is that to me?

I'm tired of being used,
Ring ring, I go, as she falls asleep,
Within a second, I am up again,
I can't take this anymore!

I'm tired of being used,
I'm exhausted from this,
What should I do?
I'm done with all of this!

Izma Khatun (11)
Lady Aisha Academy, Barking

People Hate Pineapple On Pizza

Some like me,
Some hate me,
I'm syrupy sweet when you eat,
But people think I'm not so sweet when I'm eaten on...
Pizza.

They say mean stuff about me,
Like I'm revolting, and yuck!
They even say I'm worse than duck.
Pineapple's my name,
And all fruit aren't the same,
But I'm the hated one.
They wish they could destroy me with the heat of the sun.

They wouldn't dare to do this,
'Cause they know people find me bliss.
What do you think?

Halima Noor (11)
Lady Aisha Academy, Barking

Winter's Changes

Bleak wintry weather,
Surrounded the snowy land,
And deserted the
Innocent, thick-furred animals.

All the animals gather in herds,
The squirrels carrying pine cones,
To their warm, cosy shelters.

The furry bears in their rocky caves,
Spending the
Thundery and cold winter days,
Hibernating in peace.

The birds are sleeping.
The waves, crashing on the barren shore,
Oh, how I love the misty, winter sky.

Zikra Mirza (11)
Lady Aisha Academy, Barking

Lady Aisha Academy

This is the beginning of a new day,
You have been given this day to use as you will,
You can waste it or use it for good.

What you do today is important,
For learning, education,
Because you are exchanging a day of your life for it.

When tomorrow comes,
This day will be gone forever,
In its place is something that you have left behind.

Let it be something good.

Manha Marzuqah Khan (11)
Lady Aisha Academy, Barking

Life!

Life, born on the streets,
Woke up every day so sore,
From the piercing, cold, hard floor,
I was only four and was
Ruined to the core.
I was used to it,
Until, one day, it got better.
I had a home!
Yet felt alone,
Depressed and stressed,
Why?
I had a home!
This is life.
We are never happy.
Life is just a deceptive lie.

Halima Siddika (12)
Lady Aisha Academy, Barking

The Thing Everybody Needs

I'm the thing that
Grows on trees!
I'm the thing that
Everybody needs!
I am supreme.
I am money.
I've caused kids to die on shores,
I've caused many wars,
I've made humans hate each other
To their cores.

I'm the suitcase that
Carries the dream, I'm the suitcase
You fill to the brim, the hope
Of a war-torn refugee.
I am the suitcase who bears the cross, the suitcase the owner's sacrifice
Because everything comes with a price.

I'm the thing that gives sight,
The very thing responsible for
Your fright.
I'm the thing that gives you light.
I and only eye!

Constantinos Kandylakis
Sedgehill School, Lewisham

We'll Say Goodbye

Rainy days, they are the worst
Gloomy skies, disheartened sighs
I know the bees, they have a thirst
And to snow in winter, we'll say goodbye

Is this the fate of us today?
Should we not work and try as we may?
Must little children guide the way?
And point out the disaster in the broad day?

Thunder in a lightning storm
There are no birds' melodies today
Outside it is too damn warm
A sign of our society's decay

Most people think we are done.
But together the battle's won.
Einstein, Thunberg, Delingpole, Lawson,
All told us but them we shun.

Oh, dear! Oh my! Well, I didn't see that coming!
Is this not the same excuses that we cower beneath?
It's too late! Evacuate! I hear our DOOM drumming!
Our consequences are now coming out of the sheath!

No: a stand that we all must take.
To keep our homes and families safe:
To avoid all chances of extra emission
To maintain this peace before Hell's collision.

Who are they to meddle with us,
Mighty, powerful, wealthy, wonderous.
The Leviathan of Industry,
Who even cares about the trees?

Rainy days, they are the worst
Gloomy skies, disheartened sighs
I know the bees, they have a thirst

And to snow in winter, we'll say goodbye.

David Kirinya-Scott Lamont (13)
Sedgehill School, Lewisham

Husks

Awake, O you people of bright modern age,
Take note from the lost, a tale of the sage,
We conquered our earth, not a bound'ry we lost,
We were our Goliath, The sanctities we cross't.

The people of stars, soaring up high, we flew to the heavens no thought for our death; The pinnacle of beauty, of health and of wealth. They tried to tell us "You're going to fall". They lied. They tried. We were too far gone. Laughed we youthful ones of their incompetence. What did they know of status, rank and true power?

Now away were the kisses, gone with the wreaths;
Society's shallow heart tramples us beneath;
Razed, rent, malleable clay, O woe to he who follows my way.
Even stars, you know, will fade one day.

Deep as the void, Hotter than Hell,
The now lost warnings of a hollowed-out shell,
We cannot warn thee. Death's door we can't pass,
But listen and abstain lest society harass,

We were the morning star, proud and cold; We *were* the pinnacle, now we are sunken. The deepest harshest depths of being. Empty as void, life like a knife; sharp, relentless and not without vice. We could have turned back. We *didn't* realise; the fault of our shameless pride, the ego; that haughty spirit inside. "The unsinkable ship", we fell for its trap, Society's game, the emotionless map. A blank canvas, someone else's art, no turning back, no redeeming our hearts.

Awake, O you people of bright modern age,
Take note from the lost, a tale of the sage,
We conquered our earth, not a bound'ry we lost,

We were our Goliath, The sanctities we cross't.

Martin Lamont (15)
Sedgehill School, Lewisham

Inhale And Exhale

Deep breaths in and long breaths out,
That's the only thing I hear come out of the doctor's mouth,
Why do they keep saying that, you ask?
Because I don't find breathing a simple task.

Unlike you, my good friend,
I constantly fear my life will end.
I'm always on the run from this polluted demon, you see,
And no matter how far I go, I can never be considered free.

As its smoky fingers crawl down my throat,
I feel embedded, inside a toxic blanket,
I'm enveloped.
Its cold, unforgiving hands slowly choke my lungs,
Right now, I would prefer to be shot with a gun.

I live in a beautiful city with cars galore,
And all I hear is loud engines' roar,
It echoes inside my broken soul,
And I yearn for myself to become whole.

My medicine comes straight from a pump,
But after I take it, I still feel down in the dumps,
And as I sit here and tell you how the pollution in our world affects us as a race,
We are losing more and more time to end one of our biggest mistakes.

And so my final message to you is:
Watch out for the wonderful world before it disappears,
And remember, whenever you're feeling weak or frail,
Just make sure to inhale and exhale.

Ava Annis Klara Drew (13)
Sedgehill School, Lewisham

Because I Am Me!

I have been told to fit into society,
Get dressed, put my make-up on, look 'cool',
But is that my personality?
I have to keep slim and it's that Golden Rule.

But skipping meals and marking up my wrists will do nothing.
Living like someone else is suffocating me!
I don't have to be stunning,
Because I am me!

I don't have to be outstanding.
I don't have to fit into society.
But they will find me nauseating,
As every girl needs to be a 'deity'.

But is that the person I am meant to be?
Because I think that is not me.

I am me.
I don't believe I am a 'deity'.
We need to wake up to reality.
Because our personality is our true sea.

We need to show those likes,
The ones that were trapped behind doors,
And left us within wars,
Left us in the darkest nights.

I don't need to be perfect because I am me.
I don't need to cry myself to sleep.
I don't have to be a sheep.
Because I am me!

Maria Binzaru
Sedgehill School, Lewisham

What Am I?

To be like someone else,
You want their
Everything.
Wealth?

You want to
Crawl, run, walk
Like them
Sing, read, write, talk
Like them.

You look at them
And think...
How? Do you change?

Knowing that,
Bad things,
Are happening,

You sit in your chair,
Maybe even
Think about your hair.

While animals are
Dying
Or
The Earth
Is warming up.

I shoot through the sky,
I see everything
Through my eye.

The good, the bad
The fun, the sad.

It takes more than one,
But many,
To make you get up
Off your bum.

And for you to do
Something,
Instead of
Nothing.

Tetsuya Nicholson (14)
Sedgehill School, Lewisham

Dear Bobby Star

You think you are so amazing and better than the rest
But the thing you need to remember is I am better than you
You think that no matter what, you will always be the best
But don't forget I am Villainous Ste!

You think the humans love you and that you will rock the land
It is not your kindness the people want, they only want me
You think above every single person you stand
But don't forget I am Villainous Ste!

You think being heroic is everything people will ever need
But the world will never enjoy anything about you
You think they will never ever need an evil deed
But don't forget I am Villainous Ste!

You look like a stupid idiot with pants over your pair of jeans
All the other superheroes do that too but you just look weird
When you are walking around, everyone laughs especially teens
So just look like Villainous Ste!

You look like a maniac when you wear a horrid mask
You want to hide your identity but you could have tried to look better
If you need any style tips you could just ask
So just look like Villainous Ste!

You look like such a weirdo with that badge in the middle of your top
I know even some 'normal' people wear them but your badge looks disgusting
You look so horrible you could be seen by the police and get asked to stop
So just look like Villainous Ste!

Evil regards,
Villainous Ste.

P.S. You will never be the champion!

Isabel Harris (11)
The Ramsey Academy, Halstead

Pain

I stay quiet,
I keep it to myself,
I really don't think that's good for my health,
I wish you could feel this pain inside me,
It doesn't go away, I should know, I've tried.

There's no reason why I should feel like this,
If I were gone, would I be missed?
I take each day as it comes,
Sometimes I sleep because it numbs

This pain I have inside my chest,
That feels like I'm always stressed,
But sometimes it's hard to sleep at night,
Because sleep paralysis gives me a fright,
And in the morning I feel so sick,
And trust me, it doesn't go away that quick,
But what I do is ignore all that,
And don't tell anyone that we chat.

I want to be a child again,
Back to when I was like ten,
I felt so happy,
Completely free,
Now I feel like something is always attached to me.

I dread this feeling when I go out,
It makes me want to scream and shout,

It makes my heart beat so fast,
Because the pain is a blast.

I tell myself, "Keep calm,"
Because I don't want to cause myself any harm,
I don't know how I've been so strong,
And held on this long,
Is this it,
Is this the end?
If so, then goodbye my friend.

Jessica Goodchild (13)
The Ramsey Academy, Halstead

Any Minute Now!

I've always believed in being saved,
My family is never ever scared,
I can always imagine what it would be like,
But the feeling was definitely not the same!
Any minute now...

I never knew the hot flying ball was going to hit my family,
Or knew that it was ending!
I can always go to my safe place,
But sadly that didn't stop the fire from coming.
Any minute now...

I have always imagined what it would be like
To fly like an angel,
Well, I guess I will know soon.
Any minute now...

My family was actually scared for once!
I didn't know what to do!
Every dinosaur was panicking like crazy goats.
Any minute now...

I hid underneath a tall turf tree,
My family couldn't find me, I shouted and shouted,
But they couldn't see me!
They were in the middle of the field, all six of them.
Any minute now...

I saw everyone looking up,
So I looked up at the dark red sky.
Then I looked at my family and remembered all the good times before.
So what am I to do now?
I hope there is life after this!
Just wait,
Any minute now...

Araya Jackson (13)
The Ramsey Academy, Halstead

Why Trees Are So Important

I have been in this forest here for 250 years.
I have helped foxes and badgers.
I am a hero, tall and brown.
Someone even asked their lady to marry him under me.
But today is my end.
The chainsaw is cutting me and my friends.
This is all because of you. Yes, you.
I help you, without me you would not be here.
My life has ended.

This is my job, now I'm noisy and sharp.
I have to admit I don't like doing this.
Cutting down my friends, but I roll with it.
This is my purpose, why I am here.
I get ready, held by my side, it's time.
I'm halfway through, then three quarters.
He falls, lying on his side.
Sad and lifeless, it's all my fault.
Isn't it?

Where am I? I don't recognise a thing.
Where is my burrow? Where are my friends?
So I walk for a bit, trying to find my friends,

Fox here, but Squirrel Bill's house is missing.
So is William Badger's.
Now we have nowhere to live.
It's all gone!
It is all gone!

Tetti Hazell (12)
The Ramsey Academy, Halstead

Always On The Run

I run as fast as my small legs can go,
Tripping on every single step,
Cries coming from behind.
Who is already dead?

Screaming, weeping,
Another loud bang!
Closer than before.
How can you ignore?

One by one,
Will we exist?
This has already happened
Three times this week.
I am so weak!

The wind blows past my hair,
My legs struggling to keep up.
You need me more than you think,
We carry on this circle of life.
Would you help me?

Everything is going by so fast,
I can barely remember the past.
Why am I always the sacrifice?
I bet you're glad that you aren't!

My baby struggling to keep up,
She falls beneath my feet.
My baby, she is dead!
It's always just too late.

I don't know whether to stop,
Everyone is already dead,
The stripes are slowly disappearing,
I'm the last one left...

Ellie Chatten (14)
The Ramsey Academy, Halstead

My Superhero Mum

My mum is a superhero.
She can clean the house, with the snap of her fingers.
She does the washing, without a lift of a finger.
She helps with my work, like she's a brainiac,
and also makes time for hers.

She's a first-class master chef and it's done in five.
She knows when we want our breakfast like she's telepathic.
She does all this on a diet of only leaves!

Sometimes she's like the Hulk and I run and hide.
She's always moaning, she's got super OCD.
Somehow, she always knows when we've done something bad.
When she hides stuff, no one can ever find it.

She cleans my room in a flash,
but you know in ten seconds it's back to how it was.
She rages when we don't clean up.
But when we come and do it, it's already done!
She's the best mum anyone can have.

Although she may nag and shout,
She is still my superhero mum.

Cameron March (11)
The Ramsey Academy, Halstead

Superheroes

The amber autumn leaves solemnly shook in the oppressive mist,
His adjacent quirks of fire and ice made my melancholy mind turn and twist,
His fake smile spreading across his apprehensive face,
Then soon disappearing without a trace.
A flaming burst cultivated from his abhorred left side,
The audience tried not to gawk and stare, they really, really tried...
A villain was suddenly blasted away, due to his advanced right area,
He appeared confident, but only I could see the hysteria.
An empty breath, a broken pulse,
Through sad, empty eyes, he and I knew everything was false.
The brilliance of his icy hot aura,
Taking over the globe like an astray explorer.
A gifted flame in the land of endless dysphoria,
That is what my heroically is to me,
Forcing all the malevolent villains to flee.
Battling anti-heroes until the day we die,
Now, my super-human friend, goodbye...

Jessica Eleanor Tyler (11)
The Ramsey Academy, Halstead

Dreamer

Me. You. Her. Them. Him.
Heroes.
I'm flying, soaring.
Looking to my small city.
I don't have hero X-ray vision,
But I know when I see a hero.
The man saving a dog.
The lady beating up a thief.
But then there are stereotypes.
"Muscly man - scary."
"Teenager - rude."
Stereotypes float in minds just like air in the atmosphere.
Screams. Terror. Death.
Explosions.
Bullets.
Flying to the sound.
Blood.
Darkness.
You can save someone without knowing.
I bleed.
Look at the people you kill.
Are you good?
Or are you bad?
No one cares anymore.
"Just make money and look good," is what they say.
I'm dying.

Bleeding.
Plummeting down the tunnel to Heaven.
Or is it Hell?
Goodbye, life.
But for me,
Just think,
Am I good
Or bad?

And then I woke up.

Iris Mary Rose Stovell (12)
The Ramsey Academy, Halstead

Fox-Nappers

Horses and hounds at the ready!
The fires of the gun and it's time to run
Having just woken up, I'm hardly steady
I don't even have time to get my fur ready

Running quickly through the woods
I try not to crash into any trees
I don't look back, my chance is too good
My heart is pounding and full of glee

I turn around to see five hounds
Each one running, not making a sound
My time is over, I begin to think
But I carry on running, needing a drink

Two fires of a gun means one is dead
I keep thinking of the others who are still in bed
I know I should've helped them, I know I could
But now they are dead so my plan is no good

I think to myself, *should this really be happening?*
The sleepless nights and the violent fox-napping
Now I'm alone with no family left
And I'm too young to hunt so I'm stuck eating pests.

Erin Parry-Jones (12)
The Ramsey Academy, Halstead

My Poem

The further I trekked on this stumbly path,
The more the wind stung and no use was my scarf,
The beauty of the landscape made me stare in sheer awe
And for miles around stood the moors of the north.

But as we ventured on, I noticed something,
I glimpsed at the ground and saw an oval red tin,
It was simple to spot as it glimmered in the sun,
Its shimmering surface stuck out like a sore thumb.

And when I looked further, I realised that wasn't it,
I saw a bottle, a can and a packet of crisps
And all along the pathway were bits and pieces of plastic,
I had seen posters about litter but was it really this drastic?

So listeners and readers, I ask you this,
Is this how we should treat our Earth which is full of such bliss?
Are we really going to ignore this matter at stake?
Because action is needed before it's too late...

Samuel Alexander Farnes (13)
The Ramsey Academy, Halstead

Actions Have Consequences

One minute I am here,
As free as can be,
Next minute, I am gone,
Still you run free.

You don't even notice my effect,
You need me more than you think.
But instead, you want better things,
And I am gone - gone before you blink.

My heart is beating fast,
Faster than ever before.
It reminds me of when I lost my brother,
To your front door.

You cheer as you run past,
Right now you are feeling fine.
But how would you feel...
If I cut off *your* lifeline?

I suppose you wouldn't care that much,
Like you do for me.
One day you will care.
When I am no longer free.

All alone in the dark,
Watching the lights turn off,
I am stripped from my bark.

When you slowly lose your breath
And your body starts to shut down,
You will be thinking of me
Dead... under the ground!

Courtney Marie Sloat (13)
The Ramsey Academy, Halstead

What's Happening?

I live on Death Row,
Five years to go,
What's happening I don't know.

I have been wrong in the past,
But today I will change,
Leave the murders behind
And start a new life.

I am sorry for my wrongs,
I can't get anything right,
I have had a very tough life,
So can I apologise tonight?

I'm alone and afraid,
Have I got no brain?
What have I done?
Killed someone.

I know I should be scared,
But really I'm not,
Inside all I want is death,
I'm dangerous so just respect.

All I get is abuse,
"Murderer! Murderer!"
I cry all night long,
You didn't help me along.

I cry in pain,
I'm at it again,
Another year gone,
I know I'm wrong.

Last twelve hours,
Until I'm gone,
Love me even though I'm wrong.

Henry Dale (13)
The Ramsey Academy, Halstead

I Am In Pain

I'm in pain,
It's a feeling I can't explain.
I'm sick of this game,
When I'm always taking the blame.

I try to swallow my depression,
But it comes back and shoots me like a weapon.
I try to run away,
But they always have something to say.
And again...
I am in pain,
It's a feeling I can't explain.

You stand there in a line,
I act like I'm fine.
You call me names,
Because to you, it's all fun and games.
You tell me to die,
So I go home and cry.
And yet again...
I am in pain,
It's a feeling I can't explain.

I can no longer see a light at the end of the tunnel.
All I see is darkness.

Day after day, I fight.
Maybe one day you will understand.
Maybe one day you will be in pain,
With a feeling you can't explain.

Lily-Rose Collins (13)
The Ramsey Academy, Halstead

Life Of A Fly

On one cold night, the shiny stars did shine,
The big, bold, bright streetlights glimmered into the cold, cold night.
And in a small corner that no one could see,
There lived a small fly as small as a pea.
He fluttered his wings and went into flight,
Then he flew away into the cold dark night.
The sky looked melancholy, clouds soared by,
The beginning of the day was about to arrive.

The fly was hungry and continued to fly,
Nothing could stop him otherwise he could die.
Next to a window laid a fruity winter pie,
He realised his chance and continued to fly.
He sat next to the pie as if he were a king.
A massive smile grew upon his face,
Then all of a sudden, a wind began to come near,
A colossal wind was driving it here.
His massive smile was wiped off his face
And the small, little fly was wiped out of his race.

William Couttie (12)
The Ramsey Academy, Halstead

The Original Six

When I'm walking around, I see them,
The super six, running around saving the day,
There's no worry when you see them and go, "Hey!"

Captain America with his mighty shield
Only he can wield.

Iron Man flying around,
Blasting his enemies all around.

Thor with his mighty hammer,
He'll throw it at you and it will come back at you,
Try to lift it, you won't be able to
Because only he can wield.

The Hulk, one of the strongest of them all,
Don't make him angry because you'll regret it all!

Hawkeye with his bow, he's a sharp shooter,
He won't miss a target at all.

Black Widow, she's a stealthy spy,
She can penetrate any enemy base and no one will know.

These are the super six,
The original,
The powerful.

Jacob Cutts (11)
The Ramsey Academy, Halstead

My Life As A Pumpkin

In a shop, happy and warm,
With my fellow friends
When suddenly, I get dropped
Into someone's sticky hand.
I get pushed onto the counter,
Feeling second-hand,
Then I hear a beep!
And get put into a plastic bag.

We travel through wind and rain,
Then I see a knife
And seconds later I am in someplace strange.
Oh, very sharp which kinda scares me
And makes me feel very small.

They pull out my lungs
And all my insides,
Then light a candle
And make me feel like a radiator.

I'm put outside on a speck of mud
And get stood on once or twice
By some very large feet,
Do you feel sorry for me?
I do well hope so.

I hear little giggles
And little sniggers too,
Are they laughing at me?
If I didn't feel small before,
I certainly do now.

Sophie Louise Taylor (12)
The Ramsey Academy, Halstead

A Day In The Life Of A Chocolate Bar

I feel my body melting,
Over the warmth of the heating.
Waiting to be eaten,
While a child's hunger is finally beaten.

There goes my sister,
Oh, how I'll miss her.
Sitting on the shelf,
I can only talk to myself.

My life will end with a bite
And it will be quite a fright.
Here comes a woman now,
She looks a bit foul.

This is my moment,
I can't make another movement.
Her hand clutches me tightly,
Can we just get this over with quickly?

She pays my fee,
Still holding me.
We walk into the car park
When a dog starts to bark.

"I'm going to enjoy eating you," she says,
As she rubs her head.
She soon unwraps me
After rummaging through her bag for her key.
She takes a bite
And that is where I lost my sight!

Tegan Jackson (12)
The Ramsey Academy, Halstead

Incy-Wincy Spider

Crawling through the grass and rocks,
When a great house appears in front of me,
I find a way inside,
All warm and cosy in my tucked-up corner,
I make my web but I see an intruder,
She cups me up and throws me out,
Hurting my legs but I come back,
Back in the warmth of the house,
Perhaps a different corner.
Argh, a child now finds me and is very frightened,
He squeals, "Mother, Mother!"
And calls me ugly,
I try fleeing away but she has caught me again,
Now I am trapped in a glass,
Watching them stare at me,
The cruel humans chop the ends of my legs off, making me bleed,
I try to escape, crawling but slipping, panicking,
Their father gets home,
Letting me out of my cage, back into the wild,
I scrummage away and never come back.

Harry Clark (12)
The Ramsey Academy, Halstead

My Crazy Life

My mum met my dad and had me,
Hi, I'm Ella and my life is kinda crazy.

I have a sister who I hate
Yet love at the same time (it's a sister thing)
She's obsessed with some slime thing
But all I'd like is a chicken wing!

My brother is so annoying,
He walks, runs, skips and shouts
Wherever and whenever
Just to do a TikTok!
But me, being his older sister,
I take the mock.
Then, as soon as you know it,
There are flying clocks!

My dogs, there are two
And they're cuter than you
I love them, they're my absolute world
Black and white fluffballs, curled.

Every day I come home from school
I try to keep my cool
For this family is crazy
And I'm really lazy.

Ella Masterson (15)
The Ramsey Academy, Halstead

Cruel Earth

I have ten minutes
Ten minutes
Till I leave my life behind, face the horrors of the war.

I have two minutes now
Two minutes
Till I'm going to cry.

Now is the time
The time
I leave my life behind.

I couldn't believe my ears
It nearly brought me to tears
She was saying goodbye.

The train was as packed as a bee's nest
Swarming with sobbing children.

When I arrived
The train station was full
With ambitious parents waiting
To take on the children of the war.

The bell rang and rang
I was terrified, oh so terrified
I couldn't feel my legs
I couldn't move
I was mortified.

I've got ten seconds now
Ten seconds
Till I leave this cruel Earth.

Tallulah-Mae Kelsey (13)
The Ramsey Academy, Halstead

Spider-Man

My name is Spider-Man,
I save the day from the sinister six.
I beat up bad guys who are mean
And who can shoot out beams.
My mentor is Iron Man
He is friends with the guy named Stan.
I fought with him against Captain America, we stood tall,
But we didn't win the brawl.
I met him again when I thought I was cool
Trying to stop a boat losing its hull.

I met him again when a wizard was in trouble,
I thought we were going to hit rubble
I was right, but we bit the dust instead of the rubble.
I am dead, trapped in a soul,
But I am back fighting the guy who turned me into nothing.
I lost my mentor but kept on going
Hoping to become the next hero.
But Mysterio revealing my identity
I must go on the run like Captain America!

Ellis James Owen Clark (13)
The Ramsey Academy, Halstead

Sexuality

Sexuality,
It's a major part of you and me
But when people like you and I
Are put into the public eye
We are pushed aside or thrown to the streets,
Left to fight the jaws of defeat.

We will not go down without a fight
Not until we see the light that shines bright
And lets us free.

Many generations have fought to be a part
Of something ever so brilliant
When others who never understand
Try to put us down.

We endlessly flood the streets
There is laughing and singing
While those who protest shout from the wings
We rise up, rise up
With our eyes up.

We will not go down without a fight
Not until the day turns into night
We stand tall upon a pedestal
We will not let each other fall.

Erin Eva Rose Smith (12)
The Ramsey Academy, Halstead

My Evil Plan

This poem is all about me,
My name is Dylan,
All I ever wanted to be
Was a super cool villain.

Step one was to find a lair,
I found the coolest cave,
It was already home to a bear,
But it's okay, he's now my Minion, Dave.

Step two was to work on my power,
All I needed was an amazing cloak,
It makes me go invisible
So I can scare all the old folk!

Step three was to come up with a genius plan,
It was to steal a million,
As well as to work on my tan!
Luckily, Dave is so clever
That he could drive my dad's van.

Halfway to the Gold Coast,
I thought of Mum,
She would feel rather glum,
After all, she would miss her Dylan,
But that's what it takes to be
A super villain!

Anthony Cook (11)
The Ramsey Academy, Halstead

In The Eyes Of A Football

I used to have a great life,
But even today, in a bush outside of Wembley, I lay.

I have been kicked by some memorable names,
Suárez, Ronaldo, even Zidane.

But of all the kicks, the most memorable one?
Well, it'll have to be when Courtois kicked me right up the bum!

As I flew through the air, the crowd shouted, "Oof!"
And a few seconds later, I landed in a bush.

Straight out of the stadium I went, I was soaring,
Why does everyone talk about the stars? They are so boring.

And take it from me, I had the perfect sight,
The stars may be boring but they took away the fright.

I hope my family will join me one day,
I just need a good keeper to kick them away.

Brandon Jones (12)
The Ramsey Academy, Halstead

Mustard Gas

The night is silent,
As we wait for the enemies more
And then...
I hear the screams of my comrades,
As the bell rings, "Mustard Gas! Mustard Gas!"
Then we are swept away by the gas,
Gasping for breath;
All I see is death.
As I fumble with my mask,
Surrounded by the dark.
Gasping for air,
People dying everywhere.
And then,
Nothing...
All is quiet, all is dark.
Am I dead?
Then I awake.
Dazed...
My friends' muffled screams.
I climb to my feet and try to run...
But no...
I can't stand...
I can't breathe...
Is this... the end?

I hear people calling my name.
But I cannot scream, I cannot call out.
Is this the end?

Ben Turner-Downey (14)
The Ramsey Academy, Halstead

Hot Shot

I woke up on the cold hard ground,
When I felt my heart, I noticed a pound.
No one was in sight,
I hoped no one had taken a flight.

As I peeked past the door,
Something red - not blood - was on the floor.
It was a hot substance with the name lava,
You should have seen it - it caused a palaver.

When I left the military cell,
I stepped in the lava and it burnt like hell.
As I rotated, I saw a monkey,
Very hot and very chunky.

I went to touch it, my hand froze,
But it wasn't hot like it chose.
My mind started to fade away,
Just like a handful of hay.

I came back to life to find it was a dream,
As the overheated boiler gave off a gleam!

Finley Tidbury (12)
The Ramsey Academy, Halstead

The Black Rhino

Heart beats fast,
Walking through dried grass,
Nobody knows, nobody cares what I feel.
I've lost my family, lost all of my friends,
I am the last one left,
The watering hole is empty and so is my heart,
I have no chances for a fresh start.
Wandering astray, I am no lion's prey,
I trudge on with a heavy heart,
Thinking about what my family would say.
My vision starts to swim,
I sink down to the ground,
A few minutes go by,
As I lay there, waiting to die.
I begin to cry, I didn't even say goodbye.
I can see the vultures circling above me,
At least I will be reunited with my family once more.
As I close my eyes on the cracked floor,
They open no more.

Emma Eddison (12)
The Ramsey Academy, Halstead

A Broken Home

I don't want too much,
But here I am, engulfed in plastic,
Where else can I swim?
In the poor life of a dolphin.

I see you protest,
But here I lay, no space for my eggs,
Where else can they grow?
In the helpless life of a turtle.

I am home to many,
But here I stand, burning down,
What else should I provide?
In the still life of a forest.

I stand tall and strong,
But here I roam, unable to stop you,
Why do you need my tusks?
In the slow life of an elephant.

This has been my home for generations,
But here I swim, unable to stand on ice,
Has it really come to this?
In the freezing life of a polar bear.

Amy Lucas (12)
The Ramsey Academy, Halstead

E The Unpredictable

I'm E, I go by many names,
Doesn't matter what you call me, as long as it ain't James!
My many names include E the Tyrannical, E the Insane,
E the Incomplete, but I prefer E the Unpredictable.

All those stupid, idiotic losers who try to stop me,
Well, they all get the beat down to Hell and back for me with glee.
Once they come back to see my powers increased tenfold,
Even if I played dirty first, I wouldn't have to unleash my full load.

My annoying little nemeses just don't know when to give up,
So when they go crying home, I just blow them up.
If they try to fuse together to eradicate me,
I just join the mix and corrupt them until they kneel before me.

Cian Moore (11)
The Ramsey Academy, Halstead

Life Of A Turtle

A piece of me is taken when I see a plastic bag
But now it is the only thing I have
Nobody knows and nobody cares
I'm forever wondering when this is going to end.

I lay starving on a seabed
With a body full of plastic
I thought it was a jellyfish
Or something I could ravage.

Every day is it plastic? Is it food?
When I'm hungry, I don't know what to do.
I still eat it, then regret it too,
But only you can help me get my food.

Humans dine with fine wine, with napkins on their chest
While we are slowly dying, with plastic to digest
Waiting here until we're finally dead
Dying alone while humans are surrounded in a hospital bed.

Eddie Naylor (12)
The Ramsey Academy, Halstead

Alone

Locked away, darkness surrounds
My body, but also my mind
No end in sight for these long dark days
I'm all alone.

Noises never cease around me
Shouting, screaming, fighting
Even they don't drown out the silence in my mind
I'm all alone.

No phone calls, no letters, no word from family
The blame lies within me, I know
Days, months, years ahead
I'm all alone.

Freedom, a privilege I have lost
Who knows if I will regain it?
The crisp, fresh air already a distant memory
I'm all alone.

Regret, sorrow, the pain I've caused
Remorse consumes my soul
How wrong I was to commit my crime
I deserve to be alone.

Olivia Burlong (13)
The Ramsey Academy, Halstead

Day In The Life Of Litter

Yesterday, I sat in the shop.
Today I was floating in the river,
So tomorrow, I don't know what'll happen,
I will probably be in the sea.

100 years ago, I was clean,
Today I am full of litter,
Next year, you will not see
The colour of me.

Yesterday, I was healthy,
Today, I see strange-looking creatures,
Tomorrow, I will be dead,
We are suffocating.

Yesterday, I gutted fish,
Found plastic rotting inside,
Today, I gutted fish,
Found plastic rotting inside.

This is what happens
When litter is thrown in the sea,
The fish suffocate,
Is this what you want to happen?

Katie Elsey (13)
The Ramsey Academy, Halstead

End Game

My name is Thor
I'm 1004
I was lightning from the sky
Little did you know you were gonna die
Couldn't fulfil your death hunger
So you clicked your purple ragged finger
Said you were inevitable
Couldn't even be creditable
So you turned 50% invisible
Beheaded you with my lightning stormbreaker axe
You were dead, you were gone, those were facts.

You're just a big purple grape
You tried to escape
To the landscape
You better reshape!
You got all six stones
Thought you had the universe's throne
But then the Avengers came
About to fight 'cause it's the Endgame.

Jack William Lewis (11)
The Ramsey Academy, Halstead

Who Am I?

I'm an orange ball,
Probably the size of a football,
I'm not very tall,
There is only one day of the year I'm cool.

I grow and grow,
This time I was very slow,
Then I got picked,
Hip hip hooray!
I thought it was my lucky day,
Until I get stabbed and had all my insides taken out,
Organ by organ.
I have feelings you know!

You stabbing through my skin
Hurts me more than when I play Fortnite.
I'm a bore on that.

Please stop what you're doing,
Please, I beg,
You might as well kill me instead.

Sitting on a doorstep,
Burning by a candle.

Who am I?

Zachary Dale (12)
The Ramsey Academy, Halstead

Avengers Unite

Thanos, evil and strong,
Clicking his fingers and half our population gone.
His purple and muscular skin glinting in the light,
Bashing and crashing all through the night.

On his hand, he has a gauntlet,
This is full of some powerful stones.
One controls reality,
One controls the soul,
And one controls the mind... Uh-oh.

Suddenly, we came (the Avengers), ready for action,
We told our men to cause a distraction.
We run forwards, ready to fight,
Killing his men with all of our might.

Bang, crash, boom!
The win is in sight.
The final push,
Yes, we won the fight!

Isabelle Talbot (11)
The Ramsey Academy, Halstead

Leave Me Be!

As I flew through a desolate sky,
I could not believe my eyes.
What was my home is now no more,
But a pile of logs and dust on the floor.

I remember a lot time ago,
Before they came to take my home,
The sun was bright,
The weather was nice,
But now it's too hot for us to survive.

There used to be a massive lake,
Where animals used to come and play,
Where we used to drink and sit
Is now nothing but a pit.

I don't get why they take the trees,
The thing that gives us the air to breathe.
I don't know when they will see,
They're killing themselves,
Not just me.

Brooke Sparks (14)
The Ramsey Academy, Halstead

Paper

Some people may think I'm plain,
But really I have lots to say,
Choose the colour or add lines,
I can express your feelings in so many ways,
Cut me, fold me, scrunch me up.

Born from the branches of nature,
Living so many lives,
I'm cherished, burnt or thrown away,
Cut me, fold me, scrunch me up.

As a newspaper, I spread the word,
As a book, I release your imagination,
As a card, I pass on your message,
Cut me, fold me, scrunch me up.

I help you communicate
With symbols, words or drawings,
No matter how far away you are,
Cut me, fold me, scrunch me up.

Ashleigh Taylor-Green (12)
The Ramsey Academy, Halstead

Isolated From The World

Worried, scared, anxious,
I feel isolated from the world

Freak, stupid, disgusting
The words are drilled into my head

I'm hiding in the corner
The people walking past me
Don't give a second glance

Giggling voices fill my head
Words are said that I can't forget

Huddling in a corner
Crying every night

Nobody cares because nobody knows
What it is like to feel so alone

They always manage to find an error or mistake
Something that is just not quite normal

The things they say, the things they do
Leave another scorch mark to stay forever.

Brooke Page (13)
The Ramsey Academy, Halstead

Darkness Is A Mystery

I am the thing that haunts people's nightmares
I am the thing that floods your room with horror and fear
I am the thing that can make you think about terrifying things
I can hide misery
I can hide mystery
I can see things that no one will know
I can unsee things that no one will know
I smile at children when they sleep
I frown at children when they are scared
I am sad that they're scared of me.

Some people like me
Some hate me
Some are intimidated by what I can hide
Some are surprised and happy at what I can hide
Who knows?

I am darkness
And I am mystery.

Grace D. J. Rawlings (12)
The Ramsey Academy, Halstead

Are They Okay?

Day after day,
Hour after hour,
Minute after minute,
Why does this happen?

Thousands of people
Come running into my room,
Waiting for the solutions to their problems.
Why innocent people?

As I leave for work,
Thoughts flood into my mind.
What if there was nobody to help?

Every night I am capable of lying in my bed,
Knowing everything is going to be fine.
Knowing that me and my family are perfectly safe.
What about *them*?

Sometimes I can't sleep,
I feel the pain they feel,
I know what they are going through.
Why so much pain?

Rubee Ceri Creighton (12)
The Ramsey Academy, Halstead

The Feared But Fearful

Haiku poetry

Round and round I race,
Trying to find a way out.
This place is like Hell.

Wake up, eat, walk sleep,
It's always the same routine.
I need something new.

Whenever I wake,
I hope I am somewhere else,
But my hopes aren't true.

Eating is the best,
Although it's always the same.
It becomes boring.

I usually walk,
Otherwise I have nothing.
I must escape now.

People stare at me,
It's the worst feeling ever,
I can't hide at all.

After they all go,
It is time to go to sleep.
Then it's a new day.

Katie Rose (12)
The Ramsey Academy, Halstead

Not Applicable
Haiku poetry

Elephants slaughtered
Swiped from their surroundings
Happiness no more

Torn from family
Cheetahs fighting to survive
Happy days long passed

Money makes profit
That's all I can care about
All those stupid things

So-called animals
Can't even dodge a bullet
Well, it is my job

Animals long gone
Extinction is beginning
I am helping it

Part of bigger things
My life means nothing better
World turned upside down

I cannot save them
Die, they cannot save me now
Gunshot and firing...

Animals no more.

Miles Maher-Blyton (12)
The Ramsey Academy, Halstead

Tony Stark (Iron Man)

Childhood to adulthood you were by my side,
Gave me a place to hide,
To lose myself when I got tough,
For all that I can't thank you enough.

My world has been so much brighter
Since that May,
You lit up the screen
And saved the day.

It's crazy to see
How much we grew,
In these eleven years
Of loving you.

It seems like a thousand years ago
Since all the years began
With you, the one and only
Iron Man.

I guess part of the journey
Is the end
So thanks for everything
My dearest friend.

Bradley Chapman (13)
The Ramsey Academy, Halstead

Batman

I am the Dark Knight,
Protecting my city in the darkest nights,
From inside the shadows,
Fighting is as easy as hanging in gallows.

The Joker's got nothing on me,
He's as easy to squash as a pea,
Meant to be scary,
But he's about as sinister as a fairy!

His henchmen are just as bad
And look ever so bland,
They stand there clueless, weapons in hand,
All they know is they're already damned.

I've got money for days,
Stored away in my secret Batcave.
So tell me, Joker, what's a rivalry
When there's no competition entirely?

Sonny Stokes-Shinn
The Ramsey Academy, Halstead

Gold Medals Stop Haters

Sweat running through my veins,
Silence struck out from the crowd,
Gold is in my sight,
But are my muscles just too tight?
The track is my home,
Maybe it's time to prove them haters wrong.

A moment has passed,
Hitting the finish line and luckily not last,
Cheering and booing from the crowd,
The fastest athlete in the world,
All my energy put in a race,
To stop bullying and start a pace.

A chat or two
Comes to you
While haters stop and think,
They realise they were wrong,
Cheering, no booing,
Medals clatter together as they go on my neck!

Natalie Pepper (13)
The Ramsey Academy, Halstead

A Superhero

I'd like to be Superman
And then I could fly,
Next time you're on a plane,
You might pass me by.

I could be Batman
With Robin next to me,
Driving round Gotham City,
Happy as can be.

If I had a magic hammer,
I could become Thor,
So next time I have a fight,
I'll knock them to the floor.

I could be Poison Ivy
And cast a sleeping death,
So next time someone messes with me,
They'll wish it was someone else instead.

Or maybe just being
A human like me,
I've got a lot of power,
Just you wait and see.

Holli Dixey (11)
The Ramsey Academy, Halstead

Our Names

Everybody has a name
Some are different
Some are the same
Some are short
Some are long
But I like my name
My name is special
I like my name
It is who I am

My name is who I want to be
My name is my speciality
My name defines me
My name is who I am.

But my name is just a word.
It is not my definition
I am kind and caring
That is my definition.
That is me.

Why should our names be everything?
They are not.
Think to yourself, why are you here?
Not because of your name.
You are more powerful than just a name.

Hannah Jacob (12)
The Ramsey Academy, Halstead

I Am The Champion

The time is right,
I must fight
For my country,
But also for victory,
I take a deep breath and present to the judges,
Who are staring into my eyes, waiting for me to begin,
I breathe out and step onto the floor,
I have practised it so many times I don't need to think...
It was all over quick,
I look up at the screen anxiously but to find out
I came first!
Relief rushes through me,
The crowd cheers for me,
I receive the medal which is so shiny I can see my reflection,
I wave to the crowd,
A huge smile on my face and I remember,
I am the champion!

Katie Yallop (12)
The Ramsey Academy, Halstead

Superheroes Aren't Real

People say, "Superheroes aren't real,"
There's no one with powers like Batman or Superman.

They aren't observant enough,
But in a way, they're correct.

But there are heroes,
Not with powers - with bravery.

Firefighters, police officers and paramedics,
They risk their lives to save others

Like the heroes in the comics and movies,
They continue, no matter what.

So heroes are real,
Just in a way no one realises.

I should know,
Firefighters came into a burning building and rescued me,
Then carried me to safety.

Reuben Lovell (12)
The Ramsey Academy, Halstead

Boom, Boom!

Boom, boom,
I'm locked and reloaded.
Boom, boom,
Enemies are roaming.

Boom, boom,
Soldiers die.
Boom, boom,
Families cry.

Boom, boom,
Reload me again.
Boom, boom,
Give those enemies pain.

Boom, boom,
World War One.
Boom, boom,
All the fighting done.

Boom, boom,
Put me down.
Boom, boom,
Without a frown.

Boom, boom,
Goodbye, old friend.
Boom, boom,
Until the end!

Harry Shelton (12)
The Ramsey Academy, Halstead

Through The Eyes Of The Joker!

Batman, Big Shot, you think you're good,
But really that is not true.
You're filthy rich with no cares at all.
Dressing up as a bat, man that's just cruel!
The commissioner thinks you are doing good,
But really, are you?

You stop criminals,
But do you know what they have been through?
You say people who are desperate are bad,
But you don't know what you mean.
I am merely a good person rising up for the people you call bad.

Know, I am the Joker, your greatest enemy,
You might think you know, but you will never know.

William Alen
The Ramsey Academy, Halstead

Cry!

I cry myself to sleep at night,
Wishing it would stop.
Tomorrow it could cease,
But maybe not.

You push and poke,
You call me names.
A prison for me,
A game for you.
Someone will have to lose!

My heart was once a rainbow,
But now it's black!
Yours is made of ice
And it doesn't deserve that.

I hate you, I hate everyone,
I don't know who to trust.
Are you proud?
Are you proud of what you've done?
You've turned my soul into dust.

I'm happy now,
I've spoken out.
I've won the game!

Kacey Clements (13)
The Ramsey Academy, Halstead

The Dog
Haiku poetry

As she grabbed my lead,
She made me believe, walkies!
But should I trust her?

Turns out I shouldn't.
A nasty place called the vets!
It's not a nice place.

A really sharp thing
Approached me, I want to run.
Do not come closer!

I cannot do this!
Don't get me! Please don't hurt me.
Screech! Let me out now.

Finally, we left,
But I thought it was all fine,
Again, I was wrong.

Small little circles,
Yuck! I can't eat that rubbish.
It tastes disgusting!

Lilly-Mae Cain (13)
The Ramsey Academy, Halstead

True Heroes

Quicker than a click,
The fire goes *flick*,
The erupting fire alarm echoing in my ears
As I gradually start to tear.

Luminous, camouflaged, yellow, the dimly coloured uniforms
Surround the ominous glow
Whilst water begins to flow.

Floods of water spill from each pipe,
The firefighters gather, to do what is right.
They must be brave, they must be strong,
And we all know,
They can do no wrong.

Determined to save lives, to spare all they have,
We notice the true heroes they are,
The ones who fight back.

Holly Miller (11)
The Ramsey Academy, Halstead

Goal!

People running, running,
Getting closer, closer, closer
"Oh no!"
Another day of abuse starts in three, two, one...
The whistle's been blown,
I'm catapulted through the air, bliss, aaah!
Then...
Crash, bang, whallop
Back in the game
The cheers ascend as I am kicked determinedly toward a small net.
"Goal!" I hear them scream
Abruptly ending when I am thrown as high as...
A tree
Oh no, I'm stuck!
Cries from below but I'm safe up here
Squawk! a bird picks me up with its ferocious claws
"Oh, I'm flat!"

Isobel Baxter-Deera (12)
The Ramsey Academy, Halstead

Me?

I scream but no one hears me
I am lost, why can't you see?
Where is my voice?
What is wrong with me?

Where am I?
Can you see me?
Am I here?
All I see is a tear.

I am lost
Why won't you find me?
Who am I meant to be?
Why can't I see?

What is wrong with me?
Why can't I see?

I am all alone
No one is ever home
I look in the mirror and there is no me
All I see are people who don't want me to be me

Why can't you see
I am me.

Izzy Willsher (13)
The Ramsey Academy, Halstead

The Struggles Of Being Poached

I'm an Amur Leopard,
Sitting in the desert alone.
My friends poached,
Waiting to be killed,
I might as well not exist.

I wish all my friends were here
For when things got tough.
Because I am a beautiful creature
And don't deserve the life I live.

I'm spotty, black
And have an astonishing pattern on my coat.
But sometimes I think that no one appreciates it
Or cares about a close-to-endangered species.

I must keep strong,
Fight my way through
And carry on doing what I'm doing.

Darcey Hurst (12)
The Ramsey Academy, Halstead

The Listener

Lewis Capaldi's music is powerful and bright,
He sings about love and hate,
Coming and going.
Lewis Capaldi's song titles are different...
Someone you loved,
Bruises,
Hold me while you wait,
Hollywood,
One,
Forever,
Climb,
Grace.
They are all about people he wanted or thought he needed
But couldn't have.
He learnt to live without them,
That's the message I think he's trying to put around the world,
To people young or old to follow
And that's why I like him and look up to him.

Sennen Root (14)
The Ramsey Academy, Halstead

Through The Eyes Of A Trials Motorbike

It was my turn, I was ready,
Riding steady
Through the trees and around the rocks,
Over a hill like it was a dot-to-dot,
Nearly there now, the end isn't far,
Just round this tree and over some rocks,
Making it through the markers, I was not to stop,
Up the hill and down the track,
Down a dip and appear the other side,
Nearly done, now so close,
Steadily over logs and through trees,
Through the finish markers with a clear round,
We had done it now...
Just two more times to go back around!

Clara-Jayne Wicks (12)
The Ramsey Academy, Halstead

Everyday Superheroes

Not all superheroes can fly,
Not many wear capes.
Some don't even have superpowers,
Yet they are still heroes.

A lollipop man stops cars with one hand,
Firefighters walk through flames.
A policeman fights crime on the streets,
Doctors race against time to save people's lives.

These ordinary people do extraordinary things,
To help other people with problems and things,
Such as crossing the road, to curing an illness.
Without the everyday heroes, our lives would be a mess.

Isabel Turner (12)
The Ramsey Academy, Halstead

Firefighter

F lames lighting up the dark street.
I gnited fires burn the brick house.
R acing to the incident in the nick of time.
E mergency! Stay where you are!
"F ire!" everybody is screaming.
I solated victims start losing their breath.
G lass is shattered everywhere.
H eroes of the fire service.
T hey are saved! Hip hip hooray!
E veryone cheers for the superheroes.
R oar! The support of the crowd was
S o beautiful.

Alisha Kilbey (11)
The Ramsey Academy, Halstead

Thanos Poem

My name is Thanos.
I rule the world.
I don't yield,
There is no need to.
Fighting is easy against the weak Avengers.

I think we are under attack; no worry,
Come on minions, clean them up in a hurry.
Ha! They yield. I'm too strong.
Wait till the next day, they might come back from behind...

Oh no, there's Storm Bringer.
Oh wait, what is that gonna do?
Can't even kill a minion or two.
Aaah! Iron Man. Gotta go, see you
When I destroy the Avengers!

Harrison Springall (13)
The Ramsey Academy, Halstead

My Inspiration

Batman, where do I start?
You fly high into the sky,
You are my hero,
You always save the day,
You're as wealthy as a businessman,
I don't need to explain.

Batman, where do I start?
Your enemies did their best
To put your skills to the test,
They really got under your skin,
But you were ready to fight.

Batman, where do I start?
Every minute you save the day,
Every second of every minute,
You are there, saving lives.

You are my inspiration!

Jessica Gilbert (13)
The Ramsey Academy, Halstead

The Hunt

I sit still, waiting
I hear the snapping of sticks
And the crumple of leaves
Then it is silent.

The normal sounds of the jungle have vanished
But I stay, still waiting
A sudden bang erupts and fills the air
The birds fly away, scared.

I lay there, wounded and wallowing in despair
I feel my heart race and the adrenaline kicking in
I try to run but they shoot again...

Now my dying body has been laid down to rest
I may go now
My time was the best.

Sonnie Bishop (14)
The Ramsey Academy, Halstead

Flames

Dancing flames rose
Nee-naw the engine goes,
Astonished by the sight,
Firemen put up a fight.

Flickering flames spread,
As citizens fled,
Some had success,
Others, well you could guess.

Families devastated,
People seperated,
Mighty firemen came to the scene,
As a hero they are seen.

The fire was finally out,
With tears, no doubt,
But remember one thing,
Not all heroes wear bling.

Libby Bowyer (12)
The Ramsey Academy, Halstead

Life From Above

Everyone asks me,
"What's it like to live above
Far up in the sky?"

They ask me all the time,
"What's the weather like up there?"
Thinking they're hilarious,
But I don't really care.

To live so much higher
Isn't really better,
A few inches taller,
Who really cares?

I've never known different,
I've always been so tall,
Being compared to a giraffe,
It doesn't really matter.
Life from above is pretty cool!

Gemma Woods (12)
The Ramsey Academy, Halstead

Sally, The Stinky Superhero

I can make you run,
With just one burp
And my under-arm odour
Will surely make you chirp!

My bottom gas
Makes you hide in a bag
And my cheesy feet
Will definitely make you gag.

My sweat and stinkiness
And smelly breath
Will cause you to faint,
Then fall to your death.

If you need me,
Call my name,
Getting villains to faint
Is my game!

My name, oh dear oh
Is Sally the Stinky Superhero!

Eden Florence Gediking (12)
The Ramsey Academy, Halstead

Waiting

I'm full of fear,
I'm waiting, waiting.

I see the needles,
I'm waiting, waiting.

I'm being controlled into this horror,
I'm waiting, waiting.

I've been forced into this,
I'm waiting, waiting.

They're going to experiment on me,
I'm waiting, waiting.

I know it'll happen to me,
I'm waiting, waiting.

I'm just a rat in a cage,
I'm waiting, waiting.

I'm next.

Beth Stinson (13)
The Ramsey Academy, Halstead

Elhers-Danlos

I am in pain
"That's not true, you're a liar."
Every step is possible pain.

Joints slide,
Side to side,
Dislocations,
Left and right.

It keeps me up at night,
It's not alright,
Why me? Why won't it go away?

I am a zebra,
We all look the same,
Yet we are all different in a way.

I am not invisible,
This is Elhers-Danlos
And it won't go away.

Jessica Thomas (15)
The Ramsey Academy, Halstead

Hunter Being Hunted

The hunter was coming,
He was not in a good mood,
Trying so desperately to bring back the fur of vulnerable animals
With his long-barrelled gun.
But one he desperately wanted,
The one that would get him the most money...
The wolf.
The pack hunter.
But not in this situation, this was a lone wolf,
Searching for scraps the others left behind,
Cautiously making no wrong step...
Crack...
Bang...

Fletcher Henry Walls (12)
The Ramsey Academy, Halstead

Three Seconds

Being chased down an alley
I thought it was the end of my life
Being stabbed in my stomach
Several open wounds to my leg
Bleeding out
Bleeding out
Me lying there on my own
I thought I was dead for three seconds.
Started to lose sensation in my leg
All I saw was several people surrounding and a pool of blood
Only cowards carry knives.
This is the end of me
Of my fast tragic life.
Beeeeeep...

Zac Liley (15)
The Ramsey Academy, Halstead

Just An Ordinary Poem

Just an ordinary poem
No superpowers at all
I'm not that strong
And I can't grow tall.

I can't shrink down
And I can't jump high
If I tried
I would probably die.

I can't run fast
Plus I can't throw webs
But maybe I could
If I had fitter legs.

I wish I had a superpower
And I bet you do too
But the best superpower you can have
Is just being you.

Joshua Clemence (11)
The Ramsey Academy, Halstead

A Survivor's Eyes

Watching the trees crash to the ground...
Is like watching time tick away,
Like watching my cubs die.
I smile through the pain every day,
I comfort my cubs: "It's okay."

I have no voice to speak my words,
Sitting here just makes things worse.
Humans say they will act,
But it is true and a matter of fact?
Watching the hours tick away...

Nature will break through someday.

Holly Jayne Van Blerk (13)
The Ramsey Academy, Halstead

Petrifying Plastic Pollution

Haiku poetry

Plastic is hated
Without plastic, I will live
Plastic's a bad thing

Hurting and screaming
Pushing through the thick plastic
Ripping my thin fins

I float to the ground
I shout for help so loudly
I don't hear a thing

No one cares at all
Knowing that I am dying
Slowly yet swiftly

Feeling really sick
Knowing my time has ended
Goodbye, everyone.

Mollie Deanna Mitchell (12)
The Ramsey Academy, Halstead

Dodo

I am just a dodo
A rather simple creature
Well, I was when I lived.

One day, a great big boat came
These weird creatures clambered out
Tall, slender, each with different-coloured fur
One even shed its.

I was curious so I walked up to them
One hit me round the head
Which I thought was rather rude.

Next thing, I'm lying on a dinner table
With all my species too!

Franklin James Farren (13)
The Ramsey Academy, Halstead

Rising Fire

In the house rose the fire,
Listening to the crackle,
It got higher and higher,
Everybody was in a sudden panic.

All that could be seen was bright red,
The room went foggy,
Everyone nearly dropped dead,
They needed a hero.

They quickly called 999,
The fire spread more and more by the minute,
They hoped that everything would turn out fine,
The firefighters saved the day.

Brooke Taylor Powell (11)
The Ramsey Academy, Halstead

Forgotten

Plastic floating towards them,
Plastic,
Eaten,
Extinct.
Plastic thrown,
No cares.
Plastic hurts the Earth.

Plastic ruined habitats,
Plastic is one with me.
Plastic dragged into me.
Plastic absorbed within me.
Plastic lost inside me.
Plastic kills species.

Plastic,
1000 years ago
There was none.
Polluting is not okay.

Melissa Argent (12)
The Ramsey Academy, Halstead

Could I Be Superman?

I don't think I could be Superman,
A magnificent, fabulous man.
Dodging the enemies,
Killing the enemies,
Wow, what a fabulous man.

Flipping and kicking
The baddies away,
Smashing and bashing,
He saves the day.

When a person calls, in distress,
He rips the shirt off from his chest.
He reveals his identity for all to see,
A man, a hero,
I wish it was me!

Blue French (11)
The Ramsey Academy, Halstead

Forever Home

I'm stuck in a shelter,
Dogs barking everywhere,
I can't get out!
No one wants me,
They think that's because I'm old
I can't play,
I can't walk much.

They look at me and they see a black labrador,
Twelve years old,
Sad,
Not going to live long.

I can play,
I can run,
Like a puppy, I can be just as fun,
Please get me out of this prison!

Alexia Mullane (12)
The Ramsey Academy, Halstead

Modern Problems

There were once birds, soaring the sky,
Now just spirits where they once were. Why?
Money solves all problems, by ending them.
Dictators with a mindset so rebellious, it doesn't make sense.
Wars, fighting over money, ending with eternal crises.
Everything you do is a choice, ignoring it is one.
Plastic, soon to be the killer of multiple species.
But we choose to ignore. Why?

Ewan Thomson (14)
The Ramsey Academy, Halstead

Thanos' Revenge

I am inevitable,
I cannot die,
Sacrificing my daughter,
To receive a prize.

I fight to the death
And I always win,
Another Infinity stone
And now I really begin.

Ending the Avengers,
Once and for all,
You may think I'm evil,
You may think I'm cruel,
But I'm the most powerful being,
That will ever rule.

Finlay Fox (11)
The Ramsey Academy, Halstead

A Serious Problem

Through these eyes I could see red
Sand was blowing in my face
It was boiling but there was a graceful wind
It felt like I was on Mars
This is what climate change has done to our planet

In the distance, I could see a vast city
It was abandoned and dry
But there was no life to be seen
There was plastic pollution everywhere
There was no cloud in sight.

Ashden Lyons (12)
The Ramsey Academy, Halstead

A Day In The Life Of A Hamster

A day in the life of me,
I am as happy as can be,
Waking up, all is dark,
They haven't even left a mark,
Rooting in my bowl,
Look at me on a roll,
Strolling over for a spin,
Running on my wheel for a win,
Going back to sleep in my bed,
I'm all worn out and have been fed,
All is over and I'm ready for a new day,
Now I'm sleeping, dream away!

Chloe Carter (14)
The Ramsey Academy, Halstead

I Shall Rise

Percy Jackson,
Son of Poseidon.
The cursed blade,
Riptide which he holds,
It has destroyed me twice.
But I shall rise,
Up from the ashes, reformed.
I have vowed revenge on Olympus
And that revenge I will get.
No more half-bloods like Perseus Jackson,
No more gods like Zeus or Poseidon.
I am the Titan Lord,
I am Kronos...

Samuel Pointer (11)
The Ramsey Academy, Halstead

Am I Your Worst Enemy Yet?

Batman, worst enemy, old friend
Batman, you betrayed me
Do you remember you broke my knee?
And now you are my enemy

You're a loner just like me
I know you're rich
But you were a snitch
Back in elementary

We were frenemies
Am I your worst enemy?
I hate you now
That's why you're my worst enemy.

Tom Robb (11)
The Ramsey Academy, Halstead

I Wish I...

I wish I was as speedy as the Flash,
I would say, "I've got to dash."
I wish I could fly as high as Supergirl,
I would be so happy that I would just twirl.
I wish I could change the weather like Storm,
I would make sunny days the norm.
I wish I was as stealthy as Batman,
I would always have a sneaky plan.

Rebecca Anne Bloomfield (11)
The Ramsey Academy, Halstead

When I Grow Up

I have a big nose, really long toes
These are the things I see
I have a slouchy posture, bushy eyebrows
That is what I think of me

I want to be pretty, I want to look young
I want to march to the beat of my own drum
Until then, I'll just stare at the mirror
Hoping when I grow up I'll look like a winner.

Yasmin Leah Hague (13)
The Ramsey Academy, Halstead

Super Dude

I'm the Super Dude
Riding trails
Heart pumping
I don't ever fail.

I'm the dude of the century
People say I'm radioactive
You should make a documentary
People say I'm not active.

Always out of the house, away
I never cry
Having fun every day
I always qualify.

Lewis Gardiner (11)
The Ramsey Academy, Halstead

Through The Eyes Of...

As quick as a cheetah,
As clever as Einstein,
As small as an ant,
As rich as a king,
As skilful as a ninja,
As strong as a rock,
As bright as the sun,
Can turn like a crane.
As dark as a cave,
As nice as a social worker,
As happy as a rainbow,
As real as me,
That's all I can be.

James Richardson (14)
The Ramsey Academy, Halstead

An End To Knife Crime

K nife killing happens 24/7
N obody deserves this
I t ruins people
F orever in your mind
E veryone feels sad

C rime is a problem
R ising as we talk
I rreplacable mates
M en and women die
E nough of the crime!

Lewis Dean (12)
The Ramsey Academy, Halstead

Does He?

Bruises, bumps, black eyes
My body hurts
He says he loves me
But does he?

Pinch, punch, prod
He only does it when he's drunk
He says he loves me
But does he?

Kick, flick
He keeps taking the mick
Pain is all I know
I wish I had a proper home.

Mia Staples (12)
The Ramsey Academy, Halstead

What Am I Eating?

What am I eating?
The cold seawater,
My heart is beating.

My mouth is scarred,
Dangling,
They are untangling.

I am put on dry land,
Away from the sand,
Where I belong.

What am I eating?
The cold seawater,
My body needs heating.

Noah Bradnock (13)
The Ramsey Academy, Halstead

Turtles

Turtles
Gliding,
Swimming,
Swerving,
Flapping.

A turtle lives in the sea,
His home is getting killed by people,
They get killed by rubbish.
I hate plastic!

Dylan Brown (12)
The Ramsey Academy, Halstead

Elasti-Girl

Elasti-GIrl
So fierce and flexible
Morning to night
She keeps it professional
She catches the bad guys
And throws them in jail
To leave them forever
To rot and go stale.

Evangeline Forman (11)
The Ramsey Academy, Halstead

Black Jaguar
A haiku

Silent but deadly
Creeping up on its scared prey
Now the chase begins...

Ted Hatcher (12)
The Ramsey Academy, Halstead

The Overseer
A haiku

Children come inside
They come every day now
Except on weekends.

Joe Maurins (12)
The Ramsey Academy, Halstead

YoungWriters Est. 1991

YOUNG WRITERS INFORMATION

We hope you have enjoyed reading this book – and that you will continue to in the coming years.

If you're a young writer who enjoys reading and creative writing, or the parent of an enthusiastic poet or story writer, do visit our website **www.youngwriters.co.uk**. Here you will find free competitions, workshops and games, as well as recommended reads, a poetry glossary and our blog. There's lots to keep budding writers motivated to write!

If you would like to order further copies of this book, or any of our other titles, then please give us a call or order via your online account.

Young Writers
Remus House
Coltsfoot Drive
Peterborough
PE2 9BF
(01733) 890066
info@youngwriters.co.uk

Join in the conversation!
Tips, news, giveaways and much more!

f YoungWritersUK   **🐦** @YoungWritersCW